Enlighten

Enlighten

Formational Learning in Theological Field Education

Edited by Sung Hee Chang and Matthew Floding

An Alban Institute Book

ROWMAN & LITTLEFIELD
Lanham • Boulder • New York • London

Published by Rowman & Littlefield
An imprint of The Rowman & Littlefield Publishing Group, Inc.
4501 Forbes Boulevard, Suite 200, Lanham, Maryland 20706
www.rowman.com

6 Tinworth Street, London SE11 5AL, United Kingdom

Copyright © 2020 by The Rowman & Littlefield Publishing Group, Inc.

All rights reserved. No part of this book may be reproduced in any form or by any electronic or mechanical means, including information storage and retrieval systems, without written permission from the publisher, except by a reviewer who may quote passages in a review.

British Library Cataloguing in Publication Information Available

Library of Congress Cataloging-in-Publication Data

Names: Floding, Matthew, 1955- editor. | Chang, Sung Hee, 1966- editor.
Title: Enlighten : formational learning in theological field education / edited by Matthew Floding and Sung Hee Chang.
Description: Lanham : Rowman & Littlefield, [2020] | Series: Explorations in theological field education | Includes bibliographical references and index. | Summary: "This book introduces selected key learning theories or models that widen and deepen ministry students' engagement and supervisor-mentors' mentoring. Its target audience, accordingly, is both students and supervisor-mentors"--Provided by publisher.
Identifiers: LCCN 2020031097 (print) | LCCN 2020031098 (ebook) | ISBN 9781538139639 (cloth : alk. paper) | ISBN 9781538139646 (pbk : alk. paper) | ISBN 9781538139653 (electronic)
Subjects: LCSH: Pastoral theology--Fieldwork. | Clergy--Training of.
Classification: LCC BV4164.5 .E56 2020 (print) | LCC BV4164.5 (ebook) | DDC 230.071/1--dc23
LC record available at https://lccn.loc.gov/2020031097
LC ebook record available at https://lccn.loc.gov/2020031098

Contents

Introduction   1
   Sung Hee Chang and Matthew Floding

1 Learning through Our Experience   5
   Matthew Floding

2 A Teaching Travelogue: Women in the Bible and the Church   17
   Jennifer Bashaw

3 Bossman in Recovery   23
   Franklin Golden

4 Walking by Sight   29
   Marc Antoine Lavarin

5 Learning through Our Stories   35
   Leslie Veen

6 Learning the Practice of Story Sharing in Community   45
   Erik Samuelson

7 We Refuse to Be Enemies: Being Defined and Connected in Israel and Palestine   49
   Marijke Strong

8 My Story, God's Call   55
   Erika Tobin Bergh

9 Learning through Unlearning   59
   Sung Hee Chang

10 Reeducation   67
   William Willimon

11	Practicing Resurrection *Katie Crowe*	71
12	Meeting My Body through the Grace of Unlearning *Christin Bothe*	75
13	Learning through Seeing and Naming: Intersectionality and Theological Field Education *Mark Chung Hearn*	81
14	Thank You for Seeing Me *Joyce del Rosario*	91
15	More Than Meets the Eye *Paulina Alvarado*	97
16	Bring Your Whole Self through the Door and Let Her Speak *Shaina Williams*	101
17	Learning through Our Bodies *Trudy Hawkins Stringer*	107
18	Cultivating the Mood to Linger *Angela Denise Davis*	117
19	The Mystery of Embodiment and Friendship *Allison Waters*	123
20	Breathing into Being: Affirming the Enfleshed Transgender and Gender-Queer Imago Dei *Damien Pascal Domenack*	127
21	Learning through Our Community *Marcus Hong*	133
22	Introducing Theological Education through the Intersection of Bible and Pastoral Care *Carol J. Cook and Tyler D. Mayfield*	143
23	Providential Friendship *Trygve D. Johnson and Tee S. Gatewood III*	149
24	Nourishment for the Long Journey of Ministry *Abigale Embry, Val Goins, Lindsay Ross-Hunt, and Sandra Monroe*	157

Notes	163
Index	173
About the Contributors	175

Introduction

Sung Hee Chang and Matthew Floding

Theological field education requires that you bring all that you are to the context of learning. That might be a congregation, a hospital, a prison, a nursing home, a nonprofit, or many other possibilities. You have probably become well aware that contextual learning is different than learning in a classroom. Your lived experience, your prior formation, and an awareness of the intersections that your life inhabits are the "text" to be seriously reflected upon. This can happen during the ministry event, after the ministry event, or for a future ministry engagement; reflection-in-action, reflection-on-action, and reflection-for-action.[1] When you reflect well, you can learn in a multiplicity of ways. That's what this book is about.

Learning is a very complex process in which a number of variables interact to move toward desired ends. In field education this includes growth toward competency, self and social awareness, and character and spiritual formation. Each learner can be formed powerfully through the educational processes embedded in the theories we have selected for this book.

Learning theorists attempt to explain why and how people learn, and the main foci of learning theories are the learner and the context of learning.

On the one hand, behaviorist learning theorists draw our attention to the learning context, propounding the principle of stimulus and response. Their assumption is that human behavior is learned. "Conditioning," either classical (à la Ivan Pavlov) or operant (à la Burrhus Frederic Skinner), is another name for learning. That is to say that all learning is conditioned. Reinforcement, either positive or negative, is an important part of behaviorist learning.

On the other hand, cognitive learning theorists, in reaction to the behaviorist approach, emphasize internal processes rather than external behaviors. Their assumption is that the learner is the thinking subject and the mind an information processor. They highlight the learner's active participation in, rather than passive response to, the learning process, which is a process of cognitive *development* (à la Jean Piaget).

In between, similar to the Kantian approach between empiricism and rationalism, constructivist learning theorists argue that the learner brings to the learning process their own experiences and (hypothetical or psychological) constructs/schemata and actively makes sense of what they encounter. These theorists investigate how the learner meaningfully understands what they experience, and *constructs* new knowledge, in the context of learning.

Beside the pure behaviorists and cognitivists, most learning theorists attempt, knowingly or unknowingly, to deal with the interplay between the learner and the context of learning. Constructivists help us to probe the learning process in which the learner understands a new context and constructs new knowledge. Yet it seems that most of them have not paid full attention to the fact that the learner's newly constructed knowledge is created within *a specific condition*. That is to say that human knowledge is a (culturally or socially) conditioned construct. The other side of this epistemological coin is that the learner's mind itself is (culturally or socially) conditioned.

The problem is that the learner's preconceived opinion or belief about a certain subject matter can function as a bias or prejudice. When the learner has the tendency to interpret new information as confirmation of their existing beliefs or theories, they experience what is called *confirmation bias*. When this biased learner gets new information that strongly challenges their deeply held belief, they experience *cognitive dissonance*. As a consequence of this mental discomfort, the learner either changes their perception or chooses to reduce or even deny the importance of the new cognition. The joy of learning (and teaching) is on the path of the former. Yet the latter path is often frequented by the biased learners. "Prejudices, it is well known," said Charlotte Brontë in *Jane Eyre*, "are most difficult to eradicate from the heart [read: mind] whose soil has never been loosened or fertilized by education; they grow firm there, firm as weeds among stones."[2]

It follows then that we theological field educators and students need to reflect on what would be called the learner's *conditioned yet constructive learning process of cognitive development*. This does not suggest that we should engage learning theories from the perspective of human development. Rather it suggests that we should engage the question of what the learner brings to the learning process (ways of learning) and how preconceived ways of learning would help or hinder the learner in a new context of learning where different ways of learning prevail.

To put the question differently: How can we help the learner to expand the radius of their circle of understanding? One way of expanding the radius of understanding is to help the learner to learn in different ways.

With help from a research grant from the Association for Theological Field Education, a group of theological field educators met in retreat at Union Presbyterian Seminary in Charlotte, North Carolina, in June 2019 to consider learning theories related to contextual education and to practice theological reflection on case studies. From that gathering, we discerned six ways of learning that seemed most important to share with our students:

1. Learning through our experiences
2. Learning through our stories
3. Learning through unlearning
4. Learning through seeing and naming
5. Learning through our bodies
6. Learning through our community

Each of these theories is addressed in a cornerstone chapter written by a theological field educator. We serve at institutions across the country and from across the theological spectrum, Roman Catholic to varieties of Protestant. As a group we inhabit a variety of intersections, including gender, age, race, abilities, and theological formation.

We recognized as a group the extraordinary energy we experienced and the deep engagement that took place during our theological reflection with the case studies. Reflecting on that experience, we determined that illustrating these learning theories with multiple personal stories could reproduce something like the learning we had experienced.

To do that we created a new genre, the memoir/case story, and recruited remarkable storytellers. You cannot help but be drawn into these deeply personal, even painfully vulnerable stories, like a good memoir. Their stories invite critical engagement, like a good case study. The stories come from the different layers of experience that you have as a seminary or divinity student, since the stories are told by faculty, ministry practitioners, and students. We owe a debt of gratitude to each contributor.

Each theory chapter is followed by three illustrative memoir/case stories for you to reflect on personally, but, for the illumination that is our goal, they are best engaged in a peer reflection group. You will have six new ways to reflect on the contextual learning that is a significant part of your formation for ministry. Brace yourself for enlightenment!

ONE MORE THING

Learning and serving always take place in and are shaped by context. As we submit this manuscript, we wish to acknowledge our context. Amid a global pandemic, ministerial leaders are adapting and learning at an astonishing rate in order to engage with their people in worship, to address caregiving needs, and to mobilize them in new ways for service.

Teams of leaders and often solo pastors are reflecting in action as they test new skills and technologies, learning from their new experiences.

Groups are meeting in online platforms to share stories, to care for one another, and to identify practices that nurture resilience.

Sometimes it is clear that prior assumptions need to be shed or unlearned in order to embrace the challenges of the day and what may lie ahead.

The directive to "shelter in place" to promote social distancing haunts the ministerial leader who is aware of those who have no place or are huddled together in detention camps or jails and prisons and must name this and seek their welfare.

Bodies (including the ministerial leader's body) in their congregations may feel a generalized anxiety, depression, fear, and, on the other hand— sometimes in the newfound quiet and stillness—find new and old sources of delight and solace.

The community may learn together new dimensions of what community means. Pastors and theologians are having conversations about the value and validity of virtual Communion. Perhaps fasting from Communion for a season will be an occasion for underscoring its meaning and a chance to deepen understanding for when communities remember. Perhaps participating in virtual Communion will heighten the mystery of the communion of saints who are joined to Christ and to each other across time and space. In either case, it is an occasion for the church to embrace the message of the table, the Gospel: "If God is for us, who is against us? . . . For I am convinced that neither death nor life, nor angels, nor rulers, nor things present, nor things to come, nor powers, nor height, nor depth, nor anything else in all creation will be able to separate us from the love of God in Christ Jesus our Lord."

Chapter One

Learning through Our Experience

Matthew Floding

> Follow me.
> —Matt. 5:19; 9:9

The resource of highest value in adult education is the learner's experience.[1]

The actual process of reflecting on our experience is not easy. "As human beings, our lives depend on doing many things without thinking about them—without pause, attention, or conscious reflection—because of the necessity of selective attention for human functioning."[2] We dress, eat, go to work, text our kids, greet friends—all without reflection, until something grabs our attention and we pause and take time to reflect on that experience.

It's often the surprise that we pay attention to—like experiencing two unspeakably moving, but different, responses to receiving Communion in a hospice room. One person responds with tears of gratitude, clinging to the assuring words, "Christ's body and blood *for you*." Another's tears fall as they experience the liminal space of *the communion of saints*, palpable in the hospice bedroom, recalling in love and hope a deceased spouse and parents *they soon hope to join*. Captivated by these two ministry experiences, we reflect on their meaning. The next time we enter a caregiving space, we are alert to how God will show up and minister to the unique needs of that beloved child of God. All the while, this intentional reflection on our lived ministry experience is nurturing pastoral imagination in us. Craig Dykstra describes pastoral imagination as an individual's capacity for seeing a situation of ministry in all its holy and relational depths and responding with wise and fitting judgment and action.[3]

LEARNING THROUGH OUR EXPERIENCE

What are some other ways we might learn through our experience?

We can learn from painful experiences. An awkward, maybe challenging situation results in a regrettable confrontation in our field education setting. An unwarranted expression of anger results. Some self-interrogation, and reflection on why we didn't deal with the situation before our feelings escalated, may reveal a growth area around conflict resolution.

We can learn vicariously from others. An early mentor told me a story of one of his first funerals. It was for a popular community figure, and it became a fairly complicated service. He managed to pay attention to all the details, preach the Gospel, and execute the service without any flaws. Except one. An important one. He forgot to mention the deceased in his funeral sermon. He did hear about that. His message to me: "Speak well of the dead, and preach the Gospel."

We can expand the circle of learning to include our colleagues, hopefully a diverse group of persons and ministries. I'm thinking here of how powerful considering intersectionality can be.[4] We can learn by giving attention to each other's age, race, gender, class, sexual orientation, and the many other aspects of our life experience when we reflect in community. In theological field education, our colleagues in peer reflection groups are this rich resource for learning that can open new perspectives and frameworks of understanding. We are in fact a community of practice (more on this later).

We can reflect on patterns of behavior so that we can engage difficult situations with greater self-awareness and understanding. When Franklin Golden learned that he was perceived to be "Bossman" by persons of color with whom he was ministering, it challenged him to reflect more deeply on his personal formation and how it contributed to an unhealthy leadership style within their multicultural context.[5] We would all like to be more self-aware so that our behavior doesn't get in the way of our service to others. This kind of learning through experience may benefit from companioning by a therapist or spiritual director for extended reflection.

We can reflect on our past experiences of growth with complicated issues so that we in turn can help others navigate them faithfully. Jennifer Bashaw takes us on a journey—with her and her students—to consider the role of women in ministerial leadership. You can read her chapter to experience the journey and reflect on your own formation in receiving women's gifts in leadership. Her deep reflection, and the expert construction of her course, model fruitful reflection.

We can learn by reflecting on family stories and experiences. Flora Keshgegian draws on her experience growing up in an immigrant home and as a child of survivors of the Armenian genocide to explore themes of hope and resiliency. She writes, "My parents passed on to me feelings of dislocation and mistrust and anxiety. . . . The stories any person, family, or group tells about its past shape its way of being in the world, in the present."[6] Your family has curated its narrative to take into account the joyful and celebrative as well as the odd and eccentric. It has shaped how you view and navigate your world. Becoming aware of this formation by reflecting, and maybe engaging older family members, can be life-altering.

We may be forced to reflect deeply because of a crisis. Psychiatrist Robert Coles, in his Pulitzer Prize–winning book *Children of Crisis*, recounts the story of Tim, a 14-year-old facing paralysis from polio. Tim reflects and assesses his situation with Coles:

> My mom says there's always hope—but you have to be realistic. This is a big crisis for all of us in the family, not only me. I got sick and here I am, trying my best to get better . . . Dad would say to us, "Where there's a will, there's a way." That's true to some extent, I guess—not all the time, though. In a crisis, a real tough one, you find out a lot you never knew. You find out what's true for you.[7]

Coles himself reflects, "I was in the presence of something . . . precious: a thoughtful person giving voice to impressive, even haunting wisdom." Our reflection in times of crisis may surface our unexamined, embedded theology and, by God's grace, yield a deliberative theology whose truth sustains during the time of crisis and beyond.[8]

We may gain profound insights, even be transformed, by reflecting on the experiences of professionals in other disciplines. Dr. Oluwadamilola Fayanju begins "Hiding in Plain Sight" in the *Journal of the American Medical Association*, "I have a superpower. I can become invisible."[9] Dr. Fayanju goes on to demonstrate how race and gender impact her personal experience and how shedding her white doctor's coat allows her to become invisible in her medical setting. She uses her superpower to gain insight and empathy with her patients and to do better work as a breast surgeon and researcher who studies health care disparities. For example, one of her research questions is, "Although white women are more likely to be diagnosed with breast cancer, why are black women 20% to 30% more likely to die of their disease?"

> In the halls of my hospital, on the dedicated research days when I dare to wear jeans, boots, and a fleece, when I can masquerade as anything but a doctor as I make my way to my office for a day of writing, I can truly hide in plain sight.
> So I do. And I watch.
> I watch the way no one makes space for me in the hall and contrast it with the small but impregnable berth my white coat typically provides. I watch the way that students and residents continue their beelines in my direction, assuming I will be the one who swerves when the time comes. I watch the way security guards try to hustle me along if they perceive me to be in the way of a patient they are escorting. I watch the custodian continue to mop as I walk by,

even as he stopped mopping for the young male surgical resident who had just walked in front of me.

But the people I watch most closely when I'm invisible are the other black women in the hall.

Reading Dr. Fayanju's article is an opportunity to have the veil drawn back on the experience of another helping professional and wrestle with its profound implications dealing with implicit bias and dysfunctional systems and its meaning for us.

We may not want to learn from experience. Let's be honest with ourselves. Consciously or subconsciously, we may avoid reflecting on our experience because we know that it may mean unwelcome or difficult change. It will upset the ways in which we have mapped the world and learned to engage, make sense of, and cope with life. It is hard work to reflect on our experience when it means change.

But you're reading this because you want to learn through your experience and engage in reflection to keep growing personally and professionally. You can reflect now on your student experience in a preaching or pastoral care class. Feedback you received after preaching a sermon or engaging in a pastoral care role-play situation provided you with data that you can engage to grow in that ministerial art. Feedback is our friend. Reflecting on that feedback fearlessly with others is a gift. Self-compassion is a prerequisite. Shed the perfectionism, and own that growing is human and it is hard.

EXPERIENTIAL LEARNING THEORISTS

Joseph Levine, an education professor at Michigan State University, wryly observed, "Recently someone suggested to me that we learn more from our mistakes than our successes. How does that person know? I can think of lots of times when I haven't learned from either! . . . the key is that we have the power to learn from our mistakes. And the way we exercise this power is taking time to reflect."[10]

Constructivist learning models leverage this insight and emphasize reflection on experience followed by experimentation. This is similar to what we refer to in theological field education as action-reflection-action learning. Figure 1.1 pictures this dynamic relationship between experience and reflection.[11] It also suggests that it is ongoing. We are in fact lifelong learners.

Experiential learning in the last century or so can trace its history through some prominent theorists: John Dewey (University of Chicago and Columbia University), *Experience and Education*; Eduard Lindeman (Columbia University School of Social Work), *The Meaning of Adult Education*; and Donald Schön (Massachusetts Institute of Technology), *Educating the Reflective Practitioner*, along with social worker and management theorist Mary Parker

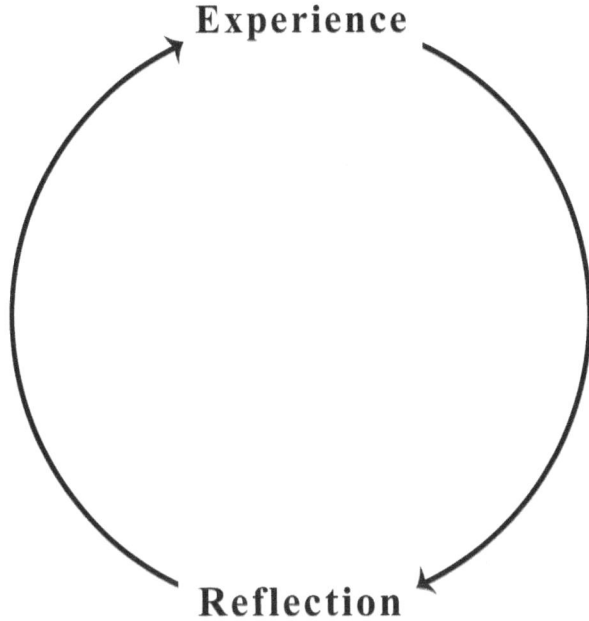

Figure 1.1. Relationship of Experience and Reflection

Follett and psychologists Carl Rogers, Jean Piaget, and Kurt Lewin. Here are three theorists (and colleagues) whose key insights into experiential learning can help us understand why this learning is so powerful and complex in theological field education.[12]

DAVID A. KOLB AND ALICE Y. KOLB

David A. Kolb, emeritus professor at Case Western Reserve University, in *Experiential Learning: Experience as the Source of Learning and Development*, identifies four kinds of abilities you and I must possess and exercise in order to learn from our experiences.[13]

First, the learner must possess an openness and willingness to involve themselves in new experiences (concrete experience).

You can probably imagine field education placements that might not seem like learning-rich environments and the resistance to being there you might feel. Jason Byassee, a pastor and professor at Vancouver School of Theology, describes his first field education experience this way:

> I owe my ordination to field education. I went to seminary to study God, not to serve God's people. But my seminary made you go and do these internships in

these little godforsaken places. I went because I had to. And I was surprised to learn that I loved it. I'd talk about God and they'd respond with encouragement. I'd visit in people's homes and feel the presence of God so strongly they should put up a plaque. I saw ministry up close and with all my senses and I was hooked. I went from an aspiring scholar to a pastor in the church.[14]

Will you enter your field education placement receptive to the formations, some perhaps surprising, that God intends for you?

Second, the learner must possess observational and reflective skills so these new experiences can be viewed from a variety of perspectives (reflective observation).

This capacity is like those nurtured in Ignatian prayer and imaginative Bible reading. Ignatius encouraged the use of imagination to encounter Jesus in the biblical narratives so that he wouldn't remain only on the page, but rather a relationship with Jesus would be nurtured. David Fleming, SJ, provides a good example of this imaginative engagement with scripture and reflective observation:

> Jesus is speaking to a blind man at the side of the road. We feel the hot Mediterranean sun beating down. We smell the dust kicked up by the passersby. We feel the itchy clothing we're wearing, the sweat rolling down our brow, a rumble of hunger. We see the desperation in the blind man's face and hear the wail of hope in his words. We note the irritation of the disciples. Above all we watch Jesus—the way he walks, his gestures, the look in his eyes, the expression on his face. We hear him speak the words that are recorded in the Gospel. We go on to imagine other words he might have spoken.[15]

Will you engage ministry events in this field education placement, growing your capacity for imagination, empathy, self-interrogation, and discerning intersectionality's influences?

Third, the learner must possess analytical abilities so integrative ideas and concepts can be created from their observations (abstract conceptualization).

In her remarkable story of encountering Israelis and Palestinians determined to live in peace, Marijke Strong discerned that the key to their perseverance in maintaining relationships was emotional maturity. Reflecting on her experience and drawing on social science insights, she reasoned:

> Being defined in relationships has two parts. First, we define ourselves when we take a position. In other words, when we say (with our words and our actions), "This is what I think and believe, this is what I want, this is what I am doing, this is where I stand." Second, being defined in relationships means that we allow others to define themselves by taking a position. We make room for them to say (with their words and their actions) what they think, believe, want,

and will do, and where they stand even if their position is different from our own.[16]

Doing this hard work of synthesizing her feelings, thoughts, and experiences allowed her to discern from her reflection, "This level of emotional maturity was completely new to me."

Will you bring all that you are, and all that you have learned and are learning, to reflect deeply on your experience personally, and with your peers and your supervisor-mentor, to make sense of your experience and articulate your new insights?

Fourth, the learner must possess decision-making and problem-solving skills so these new ideas and concepts can be used in actual practice (active experimentation).

Kathryn's story illustrates her capacity to exercise each of the four kinds of abilities.[17]

First, she opened herself to a new experience by choosing to live in Friendship House, a residential ministerial formation opportunity in which seminarians live with persons with an intellectual or developmental disability.

Second, by immersing herself in Friendship House's community building blocks—*Eat together, pray together, and celebrate together!*—Kathryn was able to reflect on the multifaceted dimensions of community and disability and how her own preconceptions about these measured up to her experience.

Third, by reflecting on her lived experience, she was empowered to articulate an understanding of participation in the Kingdom of God that necessitated leading communities that were radically inclusive.

Fourth, when Kathryn began searching for pastoral positions during her senior year, she knew how she would help the congregation understand what she meant by inclusive community. She was given an opportunity for an in-person interview with a congregation. Kathryn asked her roommate Jill to accompany her to the interview. She informed the search committee that her apartment-mate would be accompanying her. It surprised the search committee, but they welcomed Jill. Jill became part of the interview process! Kathryn later confided that this was part of her discernment process. "Living with Jill and doing reflection time together with our two other apartment-mates has so deepened my understanding of the Kingdom of God that I want to serve where removing barriers to full participation in church will not be an issue." Kathryn's active experimentation, drawing from her experiences and her classroom learning coupled with deep reflection, resulted in discerning a call. She was able to respond "yes" to God's vision for the church and world and "yes" to that congregation.

Will you exercise your pastoral imagination, drawing on your prior experience and learning, and what you are currently experiencing and learning, to engage new situations with authenticity, integrity, and faithfulness?

David Kolb and Alice Kolb continued to nuance the description of the way these abilities are exercised. They commended discussing one's experience with others, enriching the process. They noted that there is a dynamic interaction between action, feelings, and reflecting on one's experience. The Kolbs also observed that learning takes place in a context and that the context influences our learning. As you read this, you might be thinking, "That sounds a lot like field education—my field education experience!" You would be right.

Theological field education is about learning that is contextually aware and appropriate, embodied, and done best in a community of learners—and we are all lifelong learners. These observations are a good segue to the next theory, learning in a community of practice.

ÉTIENNE WENGER

Étienne Wenger began his inquiry into the nature of learning with very interesting questions: "What if we placed learning in the context of our lived experience in the world? What if we assumed that learning is as much a part of our human nature as eating and sleeping . . . and that—given the chance—we are quite good at it?"[18]

Wenger, with various colleagues, observed that learning is a social phenomenon that cannot be separated from its social context. His early research focused on learning among apprentices, and from this he coined the term "communities of practice." Communities of practice are groups of people who share a concern or a passion for something they do and learn how to do it better as they interact regularly.[19]

You can imagine how this works: a group of software engineers sharing insights as they discuss working on similar problems, midwives consulting with each other on birthing techniques, pastors sharing community stories to collaborate more effectively in addressing food security issues. If the mutual engagement is sustained long enough, significant learning can take place. We become better practitioners. Something else happens too. In a community of practice, over time, "relative new-comers become relative old-timers."[20] There is an element of hospitality. For example, the Methodist pastor who arrived at their appointment three years ago helps welcome and orient the newly called Presbyterian pastor to this new ministry context and community of colleagues.

Wenger identifies three distinguishing characteristics of a community of practice: *domain*, *community*, and *practice*.[21]

Domain is the community's reason for being. The domain defines the identity of the community, its place in the world, and its value to members and others. Membership in the community implies a commitment to the domain and, therefore, a shared competence that distinguishes members from nonmembers. A well-defined domain will determine what knowledge and skills the community will steward.

Clergy are a distinctive domain. There is a long tradition of pastoral theology and practice. The form of learning-serving covenant your field education program uses signals this fact. You and your supervisor-mentor will be engaging in a mentoring relationship that will focus on ministerial practices like preaching, pastoral care, and public theology/advocacy. One interesting feature of a community of practice is that because of its emphasis on lifelong learning in community, the learning potential is mutual. You each have gifts to give each other!

Community refers to those who engage in joint activities and discussions, help each other, share information, learn together, and build relationships—resulting in a sense of belonging and mutual commitment. Diversity is welcome because it empowers members to imagine alternative viewpoints and experiences. Members of a healthy community of practice have a sense that making the community more valuable is for the benefit of everyone.

A group of Duke Divinity students were able to experience this firsthand. The students were placed in various congregations in the same town for field education. In that town the clergy, led by an Episcopal priest, had formed a lectionary study group that had been meeting weekly for 23 years! Once the students experienced that group's vital community, each cleared their calendars for 1:00 p.m. every Wednesday.

Practice means that members of a community of practice share a repertoire. Among possible shared activities, Wenger identifies the routines, words, tools, ways of doing things, stories, gestures, symbols, genres, actions, or concepts that the community has produced or adopted in the course of its existence. As a person being formed for ministerial leadership, we might add a shared practice or *habitus* of a life of devotion that sustains the minister in their practice. If you identify with a denominational tradition, part of the richness of ecumenical engagement is seeing how each tradition nuances the way each speaks of and embodies these practices. You may even have some "aha" moments in field education when you realize, "Oh, that's why we do it that way."

Wenger insists that learning is experiential and fundamentally social.[22] It also happens within the structures of the community of practice. Not only do you become more competent; you become a full participant, a member, a kind of person.[23] If this sounds to you like the deeply formational learning that takes place in theological field education, again, you would be correct.

These learning theories inform theological field education's methods and strategies. Figure 1.2 pictures the dynamic of learning through our experiences in theological field education.

Theological field education provides places to practice ministry and spaces to reflect on that practice. Ministry is an embodied experience, and it invites us to examine our habits of thinking and acting, to interrogate ourselves and challenge assumptions, and to make theological connections correlating our experience with the Tradition/tradition (including scripture, theology, and liturgy).[24] The action-reflection-action learning cycle that nurtures pastoral imagination and growth toward deeper competency begins with a ministry experience.

Corie's ministry experience began with an invitation to deliver a homily on short notice. As he shared it with his peer reflection group:

> On Wednesday, I gave a homily—first at a 7:00 a.m. Eucharist (Rite II) and then again at a 10:00 a.m. Eucharist (Rite II with Healing Prayer). I have to admit that I was nervous. I'd only been given two days' notice, and because Fr. Jeffries (my supervisor-mentor) was the celebrant, I felt the added pressure to perform. But, after he laid hands on me and prayed over me, my anxiety began to fade. I realized in that moment that what I was about to say was, in its own way, a prayer—my words tethered to hope that God would encounter us afresh.

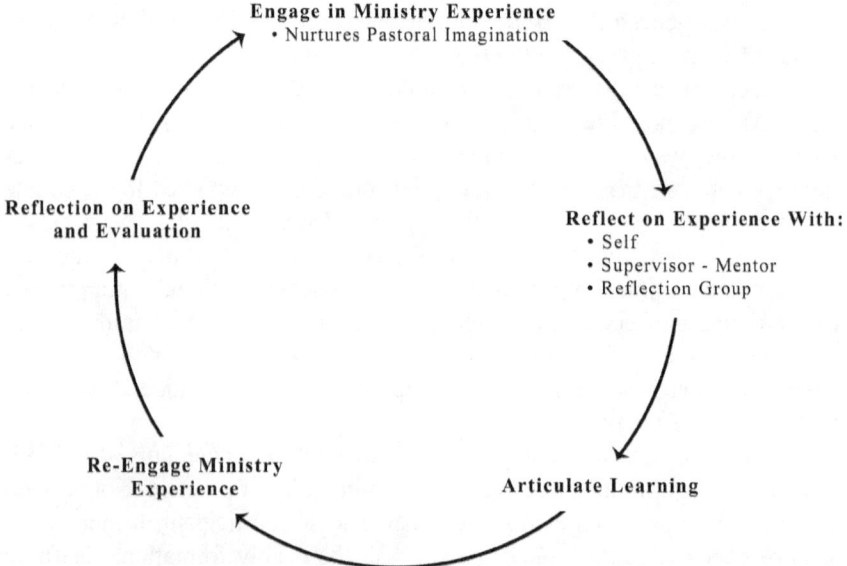

Figure 1.2. Learning through Experiencing in Theological Field Education

Any ministry event can bear fruit by reflecting on it. Corie's opportunity to preach the same message at two different services provided plenty for him to consider. Corie shared the direction he felt led to take with the scripture:

> I preached on 2 Kings 2:1–16. I began by drawing attention to the history that Elijah and Elisha have shared, likening their prophetic bond to a mentor/mentee relationship. I employed this analogy intentionally, inviting the congregation to take on a more imaginative posture, asking questions like, Have I ever had an Elijah in my life? An Elisha? If not, where have I seen representations of this kind of bond?
>
> Then I pivoted to focus on Elisha's insecurity in the face of loss and transition, pointing to his bold desire for a double share of Elijah's power as an indication that Elisha fears the very thought of being a prophet without Elijah by his side.

Corie's peer reflection group affirmed his imaginative and invitational approach to his homily. They asked clarification questions directly to Corie and to each other, like "Have you ever had an Elijah in your life?" Several of the group members then shared their Elijah/mentor story. One peer asked, "When you were talking about feeling insecure in the face of transition, were you thinking of graduation? That's kind of where I am in that story." A Pentecostal student asked about the liturgy: "What expectations does the congregation have when they come to a service knowing that Eucharist will be accompanied by Healing Prayer?" An energized conversation about how their various traditions approach "healing" ensued.

Corie then added that the encouragement and feedback he received from his supervisor-mentor between services further lowered his anxiety so that he felt more engaged and attentive, less focused on himself and less anxious about his performance during the second service.

Finally, Corie shared with the group from his reflection journal. He will explore themes from this entry later in the week with his supervisor-mentor when they meet for their reflection time.

> One thing that struck me about this experience was the stark contrast in how delivering the homily felt at the 10:00 a.m. compared to the 7:00 a.m. service. Though the attendance was lighter, the air felt heavier. One congregant in attendance was in the midst of chemotherapy and praying for their own health; another was praying for a loved one who had recently been diagnosed with dementia. And so, as I began to preach, and spoke about departure and transition, I realized that this was a community who likely heard these words differently than those who heard it hours before. Standing alongside them, I was convicted by how "out of our hands" the task of preaching is. Our words take on multivalence because God makes it so, speaking to people amid whatever circumstances might beset them in a manifold number of ways that we can never fully fathom, let alone anticipate—and praise God that this is so!

Places to reflect. Theological field education provides structures for self, supervisor-mentor, and reflection group to reflect on ministry experience to discern its meaning, to deepen one's capacity for practice, and to become more mindful of the wonder of participating in the kingdom of God and collaborating with the Spirit at work.

The cycle repeats. Corie will be a different person and preacher next time. Through these various reflection opportunities, Corie has articulated his deepened understanding of the ministry of preaching, and his own pastoral imagination has been nurtured. His peers have grown too by sharing in the formation that reflecting as a community of practice offers.

You are becoming. Taking time to reflect on your experience will ensure that.

QUESTIONS FOR REFLECTION

1. When have you experienced personal transformation as a result of reflecting on an experience?
2. How have others participated in one of your personal growth experiences by reflecting with you on a personal or group experience?
3. How have you come to value personal or group reflection? Why?

SUGGESTED READING

Colin Beard and John P. Wilson, *Experiential Learning: A Best Practice Handbook for Educators and Trainers* (Philadelphia: Kogan Page, 2011).

Jean Lave and Étienne Wenger, *Situated Learning: Legitimate Peripheral Participation* (New York: Cambridge University Press, 1991).

Howard W. Stone and James O. Duke, *How to Think Theologically*, 3rd edition (Minneapolis: Fortress, 2013).

Chapter Two

A Teaching Travelogue

Women in the Bible and the Church

Jennifer Bashaw

From the moment my Women in the Bible and the Church class received approval as a special topics course at my university, a feeling of uneasy excitement lodged itself in my being. It would certainly be a privilege and a joy to teach a class centered on the courageous contributions of women in Christian history. However, I could not ignore the challenges I would face in communicating such complex—sometimes controversial—material to young adults unfamiliar with the topic. I was going to introduce my students to a subject that demanded background knowledge spanning numerous fields of study—biblical criticism, hermeneutics, historiography, and social and cultural studies. We were going to attempt to trace a buried and shameful theme in church history through its 3,000-year development in one semester. But it was my own identity as a female Baptist minister and professor that presented the most intimidating and ironic challenge. Teaching a feminist course in a predominantly evangelical school in the South would require me to fight daily against the very system whose sordid history I taught. I would have to call upon my own experience as a woman called to ministry in a Southern Baptist church in order to guide my students through a class that would hold a mirror up to the ugly parts of their church traditions and culture.

As I planned the course objectives and student learning outcomes for the class, my anticipation and angst grew. The main course objective would be simple: introduce the students to the rich history of women throughout the Bible and in select strands of church history. The complexity entered when I considered the myriad obstacles standing in the way of that objective. The paucity of resources available from a female perspective made sketching a portrait of a woman's life in almost any century an exercise in speculation.

Also, the androcentric witness of biblical writers and historians often obscured women's contributions to religion and society. And, when it came to biblical interpretation, a hefty amount of deconstruction was going to have to happen as we studied Scriptures that had been misused and misinterpreted for centuries.

With regard to pedagogy, I wrestled with dozens of concerns: How would I navigate teaching feminist ideas to students who thought the word "feminist" was the real "F" word? How would I describe the church's history of women prophets and pastors to students who had never once heard a woman preach? I would have to be shrewdly strategic about every detail, from textbooks and assessments to classroom climate and pedagogy. I decided pretty early on that we would spend at least half of the semester studying women in Christian Scriptures, Old and New Testament, even though the literature represents only a third of the time period we would cover. There were two reasons for this: (1) I had been teaching Evangelical students for almost a decade, and I knew most of them defend their decisions and worldviews with their interpretation of the Bible. If they were going to look at women differently, we were going to have to work on biblical interpretation first and foundationally; and (2) the greatest tool of oppression used against women throughout church history has been the Bible. In order to demonstrate how women had been silenced and kept from leadership in the church, we would need to understand the original shaping of the Bible in its historical and cultural context.

I wanted my pedagogy to combine feminist concerns with a practical no-Evangelical-student-left-behind approach. Thankfully, one of the aims of feminist and liberationist pedagogies, according to Frances Maher and Mary Kay Thompson, is to help students "find their own voices in relation to the material,"[1] so I endeavored to strike a balance between lecturing and facilitating discussion of the students' interaction with the text. I was not naïve enough to assume that the students would automatically accept my authority in the classroom—as a female minister raised in the Baptist world, I knew better than that. No, I had to earn my students' trust before they would listen to me, of all people, about the history of women and the church.

I decided to gain their trust with my own vulnerability. On the first day of class, I told my story. I told them about my call to ministry as a teenager in a Southern Baptist church, about how difficult it was to envision a future as a church leader when I saw no female models in ministry around me. I recounted a fateful intervention some of my male friends at Baylor had scheduled with me during my senior year. With their nonsensical interpretation of Ephesians 5, they tried to dissuade me from going to seminary. "What would be the point?" they said. "Obviously, you can't be the head of a church if you can't even be the head of a family." As I lay my life bare in front of my students, they began to see how much was at stake in our study of women in the Bible and the church. This history had a tangible impact—and often damaging consequences—on real people in the past *and* the present.

On the second day of class, I introduced my students to the diverse expressions of feminism. For many of our Evangelical students, a feminist is still the boogeyman to them, a man-hating, baby-killing social justice warrior for the side of evil. We knocked down that straw-woman quickly by surveying classic definitions of feminism. We discussed Marie Shears's oft-repeated definition, "Feminism is the radical notion that women are people too," and I could feel students' shields being lowered. Then, we read Letty Russell's eloquent defense of feminist pursuits:

> Feminism is advocacy of women. It is not, therefore, against men, but only for the needs of women, needs that cannot be met without changes in the lives of both men and women. . . . It represents a search for liberation from all forms of dehumanization on the part of those who advocate full human personhood for all. . . . This means that men can also be feminists if they are willing to advocate for women.

They were bowled over by the surprising realization that men could be feminists too. By setting the tone with my experience as a woman in ministry and then deconstructing their misconceptions about feminism, I had successfully eased my students into a state of openness and empathy. They started to name the fear-mongering, antifeminist rhetoric to which they had been exposed, and they showed a willingness to view feminism in a new way. It was a hopeful start to the class.

Next, we tackled the biblical narrative. For our study of Old Testament women, I chose a book written by Jewish feminist scholar Tikva Frymer-Kensky called *Reading the Women of the Bible*. Frymer-Kensky uses detailed literary analysis and expertise on ancient Near Eastern culture to highlight narrative connections between biblical women characters. She categorizes the women in the Hebrew Bible, from major to extremely minor characters, into four groups—victors, victims, virgins, and voices. I hypothesized that students would interact more easily with feminist criticism that provided a close reading of the text rather than theory and that starting with the Hebrew Bible would mean less was at stake for them. It turned out I was right.

First, we learned from Frymer-Kensky about how Israel, even with its patriarchal structures, valued the voices of women enough to place them at key moments in their narratives. Through our reading, students began to understand that women's stories are mediated through the male perspective, and every portrayal of a female character was subject to contextual situation and the editorial objectives of the authors.

I knew our study of the New Testament literature would come with more baggage, so I did not pull any punches. I taught a mini-hermeneutics 101 course in less than a week, emphasizing the "situatedness" of readers and the importance of genre and social and cultural context. For our exploration of New Testament women, I selected Francis Taylor Gench's *Back to the Well*, which synthesizes a wide swath of feminist scholarship and focuses on Jesus's interactions with particular women in the Gospel. In our journey through the Gospels, we highlighted the positives in the Gospels' portrayal of women. I knew from classroom and church experience that focusing too critical of a lens on the stories about Jesus would strike the wrong chord in many Evangelical students' ears.

By the time we got to Paul and women, the students were exercising some keen interpretive skills. They read the problem passages—1 Corinthians 14 and the household codes—with proper attention to their literary and cultural contexts. Before our class discussion on the pastoral letters, I sent the students home with two articles: an egalitarian interpretation of 1 Timothy 2 and a complementarian reading of the same passage. Even though they were more familiar with the complementarian view, the hermeneutical training they had received opened their eyes to the lack of attention the author gave to issues of context and lexical ambiguity. I did not even have to point out the weaknesses of his argument about women not teaching or exercising authority over men. They did it in their own discussions with one another. It was amazing! It felt like I had taken the training wheels off my child's bike and watched him pedal down the street, perfectly balanced.

After that, the students were ready for the chaos of early church history. Barbara MacHaffie's *Her Story: Women in Christian Tradition* would take us from the early church through women in modern church traditions. It was evenhanded and accessible, and it offered a combination of primary sources from men and women authors as well as succinct overviews of different eras in church history. For our reading of these primary and secondary materials, I shortened my lectures to allow the students to lead group discussion for most of class time. As the authority shifted in the classroom from professor to student, the dynamic among the students changed as well. They began to work together to make sense of the readings. As they taught and argued with one another, a sort of democratic unity emerged.

The church fathers made the students pretty irate. We had already discussed how Roman household codes and the misogynistic anthropology of the Greeks had shaped much of ancient philosophy and theology. Then, one day they read this excerpt from Origen: "Even if it is granted to a woman to show the sign of prophecy, she is nevertheless not permitted to speak in an assembly. When Miriam the prophetess spoke, she was leading a choir of women . . . For [as Paul declares] 'I do not permit a woman to teach,' and even less 'to tell a man what to do.'"[2] As my Evangelical students acknowledged the cultural bias in Origen's reading of Scripture, it dawned on them how their own churches read passages similarly, through the lens of conservative patriarchy. By the time the semester ended, a radical change had occurred in almost all my students. They were not only better interpreters of Scripture and readers of history; they were empowered by a rich tradition of women prophets, preachers, missionaries, and scholars that they had never before known existed. My careful planning of the course—built on the experience I had gained teaching and ministering in Evangelical settings—had resulted in transformative learning for my students. They had learned about the silencing of women in the church, but they had also encountered the men and women whose voices rose up against the patriarchal structures of the church and proclaimed the truth of Scripture. I had learned something as well—what it was like for a woman who had been silenced by the church to finally find her voice by teaching future preachers and laypeople who would—God willing—use their experiences in my class to change the church for future women in ministry.

QUESTIONS FOR REFLECTION

1. Professor Bashaw writes, "I would have to call upon my own experience as a woman called to ministry in a Southern Baptist church in order to guide my students." What experiences did she draw upon to offer guidance through the journey her course took students on?
2. What do you think is the relationship among courage, vulnerability, and reflection?

Chapter Three

Bossman in Recovery

Franklin Golden

I was the newly ordained pastor of a small Presbyterian church in Durham, North Carolina, when I had a life-changing experience of belonging and love across racial boundaries. As a son of the enduring (racist of its particular kind) South, and a Presbyterian to boot, it's fair to say this is not what I was expecting. When I am feeling cheeky, I like to say that Presbyterian comes from the Greek for "really, really, really white." So, when young people of color started to worship with an older generation of white Presbyterians a few months into my first call, I was as grateful as I was perplexed.

Growing up in a Presbyterian church, I'd never seen an African American standing alongside someone with a very visible Confederate battle flag tattoo in the line for Communion. Now I was seeing this, every week, at the Lord's table. For a while, I thought this unexpected and beautiful craziness might last. But when the new and nonwhite decided to embrace the language of belonging—of formally joining the church—resistance took hold. Painful conversations about change tended to focus on the order of worship, or music, until a black woman said, "When you talk about change being hard and painful, you aren't really talking about worship. You are talking about the presence of *my body in this space*."

For many of us, the presence of unexpected bodies was intoxicating and transformative. Complicated, to be sure, but beautiful. We discovered Jesus to be wonderfully present in the surprising intimacy we found with one another and with the Lord. Others, however, didn't see new life in these new bodies. They only saw the death of something they loved dearly.

Love it or hate it, it didn't last long. The Holy Spirit defunded us. We ran out of money; the church scattered. A handful of us hustled and schemed, raised money and made plans. We jumped (and cursed) through interminable Presbytery hoops. In the end a new congregation with the most boring name of any new church development ever—Durham Presbyterian Church—was born. We didn't know what we were doing. (More accurately, we didn't know what was being done to *us*.) We didn't have a plan, just a desire for more of what we had experienced. We ended up a few miles down the same street, with a comically large church building for our micro-flock and a partnership with a Hispanic congregation worshipping in the same space.

In the beginning we liked to say we wanted to be a church "as diverse as our city." We are almost nine years into being Durham Church, and we've never been as diverse as our city. We are, and always have been, a majority white congregation—more racially and socially diverse than most churches, but still white. It took several years to realize that even our best hopes were saturated in whiteness. We had a vocabulary of racial reconciliation but not of racial justice. We were like a three-year-old who wants a tractor. Just because you want it doesn't mean you are ready. The desire for intimacy across racial lines was stirred up from our own experiences of that very intimacy, but the white folks were only beginning to reckon with the truth, pain, and grotesqueness of the ways white supremacy had misshaped us. We had to seriously reflect on things we'd never even been aware of.

Here's one story of my own slow, painful, joyful, and ongoing learning. A few years into Durham Church, we decided to hire co-music directors. One was a white bandleader, a banjo-playing journalist with a love and gift for incorporating secular music into worship. His partner in this forced marriage was an African American man steeped in the traditions and sounds of the black church and contemporary worship music. For all sorts of reasons, their partnership didn't take, and we decided to let them both go.

You can't fire a church musician without getting pushback from somebody. If you let go of two at once, it's time to go to the mattresses. Being an empath with boundary issues, I carried in my body more of the anxiety, frustration, and pain of the congregation—especially the musicians—than I realized. Because I'm overly sensitive, driven by a congenital aversion to conflict, and have a firstborn's drive to please, my sympathetic nervous system flooded my body with enough stress hormones to keep me up for days. It was like I was on pastor steroids. I crafted plans, set timelines, created new structures. When I was done, I offered the fruit of my labor to the church band as if it were a precious gift, tailor-made to banish any uncertainty, anxiety, doubt, frustration, or fear. I was letting everyone know that comfort and stability would reign!

That's when the band called an emergency meeting. When I got there, I learned the only thing on the agenda was . . . me.

We met in my home office, a finished garage with big couches and chairs, the site of many prayers, small groups, and pastoral care moments. Now I was there at the request of several sisters and brothers of color deeply devoted to the church and the music of the church. John, a seminary student, captured the feeling of the other musicians when he said, "You have hurt us. When things got hard you fell back to your default way of being. You made unilateral decisions and took control that wasn't yours to take. Worse, you have acted contrary to the very way you've been encouraging us to live. You made an 'us' thing about you, at the expense of the band, in a way that is especially painful for people of color."

John was right. I did what many tend to do under stress. I fell back on the ways I knew best. I defaulted to the way of being that shaped me without me ever really questioning it. I thought of the story an interim pastor at a neighboring congregation tells of the time he listened patiently as an older member of the congregation described the qualities needed in their next senior pastor. When the man sat down, the interim said, "You don't want a pastor . . . you want a Confederate general!" That was my default mode.

I grew up in a large, affluent PC(USA) congregation in Charlotte. The mayor was my Sunday school teacher. Each week, bank presidents, CEOs, and a U.S. congressman sat in the pews surrounding my family. When I preached for the first time, in the ninth grade, these same people told me they wanted me to go to seminary. They didn't let up until I agreed to go 10 years later.

In the world that formed my imagination and sense of myself, leaders were white, male, and assertive. They got stuff done. They had some gifts for listening and inclusion, but there was never any doubt who was in charge. There was unspoken consensus about what leadership looked like. And it worked—for a white church. It did not, however, prepare me to pastor a multiracial church sharing life with a Hispanic congregation.

When we first entered into a covenant to share life and space with Iglesia Emanuel, another new church development, we decided to renovate the sanctuary together. It was a remarkably smooth process. My fears about cross-cultural church renovation proved to be unfounded. (And I took it surprisingly well when my pitch to paint the sanctuary Pittsfield Buff moved absolutely no one.) It was only later that I learned I had a nickname among the brothers—and it was all brothers on this project—from Emanuel.

I was "Bossman."

Of course that was my nickname. All I wanted was new and surprising friendships that bear visible witness to the truth that Jesus draws people to himself in defiance of the world's boundaries. I wanted beloved community, dammit! And I was *Bossman*. Shit. What hurt more than the nickname itself was that I was *surprised* when my colleague at Emanuel graciously told me about it. Perhaps I thought good intentions and holy desires could cover a multitude of inherited sin that was as indelibly a part of me as a fingerprint. Not only was I unaware I *was* the bossman; I was unaware that I *liked it*, unaware that not rejecting it is the same as choosing it.

Back to the music. After John told me the truth about myself, that I fell back on old ways that were incompatible with our shared life, he asked what I thought repentance might look like. I'm tempted to make up words that make me sound better than I am, but the truth is I can't remember what I said. I *do* remember how it felt (and still feels) like a miracle that a black man a decade younger than me, his white pastor, loved me enough to tell me the truth about myself. He, and the others, returned the pain I'd inflicted with truth-telling love. Blocking any off-ramp of cheap grace, they blessed my fumbling toward repentance.

Several months later we decided not to hire someone to replace the music directors. We would be leaderless. We had plenty of good musicians, but the idea of not having a designated leader was scary for some. In one meeting, a musician was making an argument that strong leadership is essential for a band. A few others nodded as she asked, "What happens if we are unsure? What if we get lost somehow? Who would we look to?" I asked a question in response: "What would it be like to look to one another?" With a little bit of fear, and a little bit of new hope, we deprived ourselves of the comfort of a bossman.

We also changed our vocabulary. Instead of leaders, we had *listeners*. When a "leader" emerged organically from within the band, we had learned that those gifted and set apart for certain tasks, before they do anything else, are called to *listen*. To the Spirit. To one another. To their own hearts and the lies we all tell ourselves about what it means to be human. Listen to whispers of fears of failure, anxiety over outcomes, hunger for control. Good listeners know that competence and control are pitiful substitutes for the weakness that perfects God's power. Listeners don't take up space that just might be the location of another's joy and purpose. Listeners know we don't need white saviors—that's what we need to be saved *from*.

A few times each year in worship at Durham Church, we read together every instance of the phrase "one another" in the New Testament. The "one anothers" reveal the Gospel to be the living body of Jesus in the church. They don't leave room for an aspiring bossman or accounts of faith found outside of holy kisses, washed feet, and shared burdens. The one anothers end in powerful crescendo. Six consecutive times we say, with one voice:

> Love one another.
> Love one another.
> Love one another.
> Love one another.
> Love one another.
> Love one another.

How does somebody like me learn to love? How do I learn to *be* loved? How is mutual love even possible when you were born and raised to be the bossman? The old Steve Martin stand-up bit (borrowing from the much-less-funny John the Baptist) gives the answer I most cling to: get small. And remember *I am not the gift*. I am a bossman in recovery, learning to receive the gifts of new life that allow me to die a little every day to the empty comforts and promises I inherited, the story I was given to tell of myself. Most precious among those gifts: the ongoing recovery and repentance made possible by a love I don't deserve, offered in and from the beautiful and unexpected faces of those who are, to me, the very face of Christ's mercy.

QUESTIONS FOR REFLECTION

1. How would you describe the power of reflection revealed in Pastor Golden's story?
2. What is your response to reflection on experience that leads to uncomfortable self-knowledge?

Chapter Four

Walking by Sight

Marc Antoine Lavarin

Wincing as my physical therapist tested the limits of my pain and patience threshold, I had finally reached my boiling point. I stopped our hour-long training, packed up my things, and began to head toward the door. I didn't want to be there, and the more I thought about it, the angrier I felt. I mean, honestly, what are the chances of tearing your Achilles tendon twice within the span of one month!

Picking myself up from the carpeted floor of a not-so-well-ventilated physical therapy clinic, I struggled to add pressure to my recently surgically repaired left Achilles tendon. My physical therapist, noticing how frustrated I was, walked over to attempt to convince me to stay and complete my training. As she spoke, I looked at her, knowing I didn't want to stay while also recognizing that I needed to in order to be prepared for my upcoming summer internship.

Thinking of my internship only made it harder to hear my physical therapist. I had already told my field education director that, after a second Achilles injury, I was no longer interested in doing anything this summer, let alone interning at a prominent church. Yet after prayer and guidance, I still felt convinced to do so. But if I struggled to lift five added pounds of weight with my injured leg, how was I going to lift myself through this internship? How can I be a strong leader while injured? How will I overcome this Achilles' heel of mine (pun intended)? To make matters worse, the more I thought about my field education placement, the more insecurity strode through the corridors of my mind. Founded on the resilience of former slaves, the Alfred Street Baptist Church has over 200 years of prophetic witness, over 80 ministries, and countless contributions beyond the greater Alexandria, Virginia, community, and it is led by Rev. Dr. Howard-John Wesley, who was one of my personal ministry role models. How could I be successful while literally limping my way through my field education experience? While I was dwelling on the reasons why I couldn't complete my physical therapy or start my internship, my physical therapist interrupted my train of thought with some advice: "See yourself walking in the future." Leaving physical therapy that day, I wasn't sure how I was going to envision what I struggled to see for myself.

As God's humor would have it, and thanks to the physical therapy, I was off of my walking boot within a few weeks of my internship. However, it was the moment I took off my walking boot and put away my crutches that I realized that I couldn't take off nor put away the questions I had in physical therapy. While my physical injury had healed, my confidence was in need of much triage. I had spent months healing my physical injury, but it was my wounded confidence that needed treating. My field education experience forced me to face a call that was easier to dream about than live. In hindsight, my apprehension about interning at Alfred Street wasn't about seeing myself healed from an injury but rather seeing myself stand in my call to ministry. I used my injury as a crutch to avoid the pressure of having to stand on a vision that I had for myself but did not believe I could really become. It's no wonder I turned down the internship the day after tearing my Achilles, because deep down, I was always looking for a way out of confronting my call. Two full years of seminary, one study-abroad experience, and countless words of affirmation from professors and peers, and I was still uncomfortable with embracing my call. Growing up as a son of a pastor, I've seen my father give everything he had while never collecting a check and working a second job. My mother seemed to have always been in direct sync with God, always having the right word in her heart. It was comfortable to see my parents and mentors live into their call, but it was hard to imagine that God would invite me to the high call of that journey. Something about this call seemed to require something "bigger," something that was already in other people that I wasn't sure I already possessed.

Throughout the summer, I stretched my vision for myself, but, like in therapy, I came to a point where the stretch tested the limits of my faith. With only a few weeks left in my internship, I was tasked with preaching the final sermon of the summer. I was progressively recovering from my injury, loving and growing with the people, and now I had to preach a sermon that I felt would speak to my experience but also my calling. In the weeks leading up to the sermon, I was suffocated by the very thought of preaching at Alfred Street. Preaching was hard enough without trying to be vulnerable and crafting a sermon about complex theological issues like suffering, theodicy, and God's permissive will like I felt called to preach.

With Sunday quickly approaching, I had to fight to be true to the lessons that I learned over the course of the summer and fight off the temptation of preaching an older sermon that might "do the job." Sitting in my supervisor's office that week, I inundated her with reasons why I shouldn't preach: "Dr. Judy, we can give someone else an opportunity to preach. This type of sermon should come from the senior pastor." And the one I laugh at the most in retrospect: "I don't know if I feel called to preach; maybe I'm just a teacher." Dr. Judy wasn't buying it. She affirmed my call, assured me the words would come on Sunday even if they didn't show up on my manuscript during the week, and sent me away. Before I could lift myself from the chair and head to my cubicle, I realized that I was doing it again. I was finding reasons not to confront my call, just like I had done with my Achilles injury. I realized that I was asking my supervisor the same questions that I had been asking myself before I even showed up to Alfred Street. These questions weren't necessarily about the sermon; they were about the preacher who would be preaching the sermon. Did I truly believe that God called me? Did I envision myself being the person God called me to be? Was I willing to go where God called me?

Leaving my supervisor's office that day, I was reminded of my field education director's words of rebuke when I initially turned down my offer to intern at Alfred Street after tearing my Achilles tendon for the second time. She told me, "Marc, you're supposed to be there." Sitting in my cubicle, with my head in my hands, praying but also tearfully feeling sorry for myself, it dawned on me that I wasn't allowing my field education director's words to sit with me. She told me, "Marc, you are supposed to be there." All this time I had been placing an emphasis on the "there" and completely ignoring the "you." For so long I had been allowing the painful process of healing to shape my "you" instead of allowing me to shape the "there." God wanted me there, and if God wanted me there, God would utilize all of me, in whatever state I was in—injured or completely healed—physically and spiritually.

What was making my call difficult to live into is the lack of vision for who I am and who I shall be. I've learned that we live into our calls the most when we show up as we are and allow the journey to shape us into who we will become. Afraid of confronting my own call story, I tried to live into it by portraying the characteristics I thought were necessary to become "successful" in ministry. I thought I had to be strong, and to seem smart, and to perform perfection. In reality, what I needed was to be true to myself. We commit violence against our call narratives when we choose to become different characters in our own story. When we allow past injuries to prevent us from occupying space we've been called to walk in, we ignore the truth that even post-resurrection comes with scars. There are times when, like David, we need to hand Saul back his armor (the shields we place over our authentic selves) and take up our slingshot and stones, because although they may not be the king's armor, they've been tested through the school of experience.

My field education experience was teaching me how to walk again, not physically but ministerially.

The morning of the sermon, I woke up from a few hours of sleep with the realization that my sermon manuscript was still incomplete. Sliding off of my bed and onto my knees, I began to pray that God would fill in the words that were not on my manuscript. I got off my knees and onto my feet quicker than I normally would and was overwhelmed with a sense of confidence. I didn't have confidence in my sermon as much as I did about my placement, that I was where I was supposed to be. I wasn't sure how the sermon was going to go, but I was sure that I was going to where I was supposed to be. As can be expected of God, the sermon went better than I could have ever imagined. People gave their lives to Christ and joined the church, and a few congregants asked to receive prayer, thanks be to God. However, the highlight of my 11-week experience came at the very end of that service. I was asked to stand at the back of the church to shake hands with the congregants as they left the sanctuary. As the line started to wind down, a little girl walked up to me and handed me a piece of paper. "This is for you," she said with the sweetest voice. She had drawn a picture of me standing in the pulpit, preaching. Many people would have passed over this as a cute but ultimately insignificant moment. But, to an intern struggling to look his vocation in the eye, it took a little girl's drawing to help me see myself for who I am.

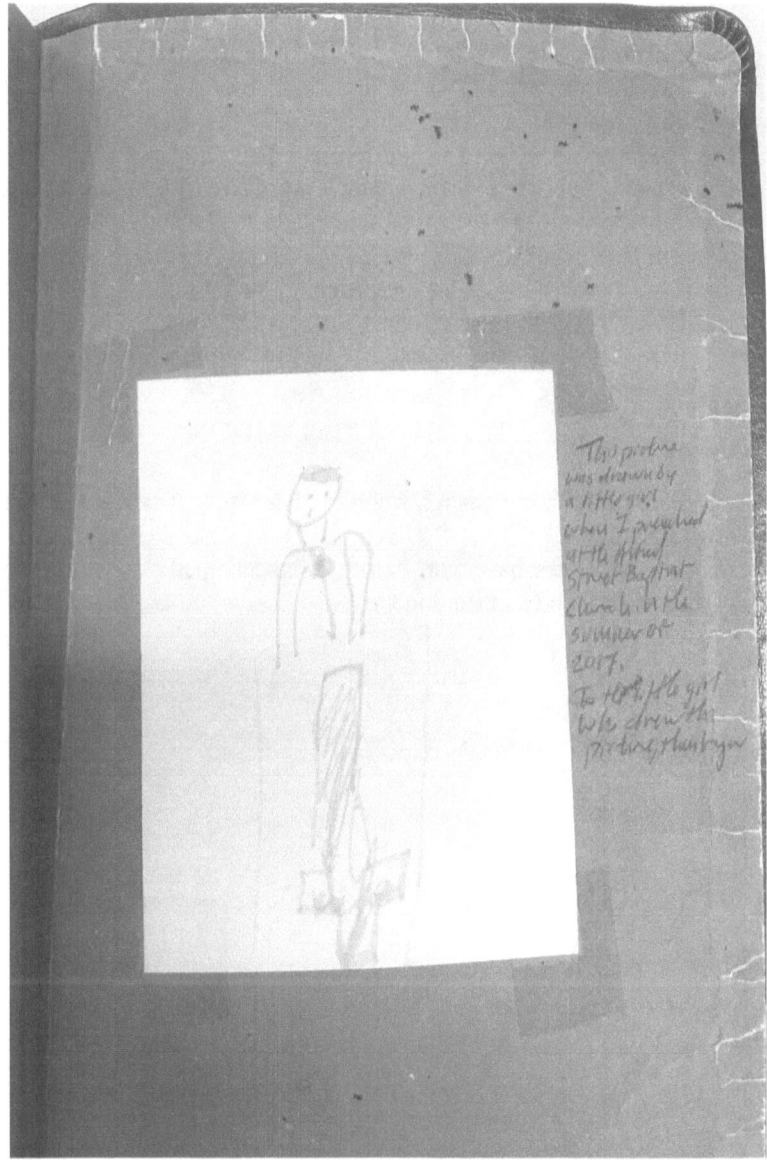

Figure 4.1. Little Girl's Portrait of Author Text reads, "This picture was drawn by a little girl when I preached at the Alfred Street Baptist Church in the summer of 2017. To the little girl who drew the picture, thank you."

Her drawing not only showed me myself but also allowed me to recognize all the people who had helped me to see myself and had walked with me when it was hard to walk—the people who saw me and loved me too much to allow me to utilize them as my crutch but forced me to walk the excruciating journey of self-discovery. While God calls us individually, our calls are also communal. Many times it takes the vision of another to see beyond what we can believe. This little girl's drawing allowed me to understand my field education director's words: "I was supposed to be here." This little girl's drawing allowed me to appreciate my physical therapist's words that I needed to "see myself walking in the future." This little girl's drawing allowed me to believe my supervisor-mentor's words of affirmation. This little girl's drawing affirmed the promises God made to the little boy inside of me—the promise to walk alongside me all the days of my life. That moment, I promised that I would never let the prophecy of this little girl's drawing down. I quickly taped it to the back sleeve of my preaching Bible so that this little girl's prophecy would be fulfilled every time I stood to preach.

QUESTIONS FOR REFLECTION

1. As Marc Lavarin curates his Achilles' heel story, where does he find God showing up?
2. What experiences have you had that have helped you discern your Achilles' heel and its meaning?

Chapter Five

Learning through Our Stories

Leslie Veen

> The meaning of the world and of our experience is not given in advance, and the task of knowledge is not merely to discover this given. Rather, the perceived world imposes a task to be accomplished, which is to make out of what is given something meaningful.
> —Donald E. Polkinghorne, *Narrative Knowing*[1]

But what does it all mean?

How often are we left sitting with that question? Leaders of faith communities are approached with such questions weekly, if not daily. Faith is supposed to be the ultimate meaning maker, the thing that will bring all the disparate pieces of our lives together, the thing that will make it all feel like it has some kind of value, that it all should be waded through no matter how thick or deep it (the stuff of life) gets.

What does it all mean?

MEANING MAKING

This is a question that you, who are ministerial leaders-in-training, are asked to contemplate and answer as you go about the practice of ministry in a supervised setting. For many of you, that question may be off-putting, confusing, even threatening. For much of your educational experience, the focus probably hasn't been on meaning making so much as on information gathering. As you progressed through the ranks of educational systems, you were probably increasingly asked to begin to make meaning out of the pieces of information that you acquired. And so, you came to your Supervised Ministry setting with some practice at this activity. And yet, you may still feel ill-equipped to answer the question for yourself, let alone for others.

By the time people reach graduate-level education, they approach the learning in their degree program with certain expectations for how information will be presented, how that information will be learned, and how they might go about integrating that information into their own worldview. In such settings, most expect that success will largely be measured by how well they master the information given and, to a lesser extent, by how they integrate it into their existing knowledge to give them a more wholistic worldview. These expectations often get turned on their head when embarking on the learning experience of Supervised Ministry.

Gone are the typical markers of higher education—textbooks, lectures, final papers, and projects demonstrating learning in a course. Gone are the more rigid external expectations set by the course's professor of what should be learned through the coursework. Gone are the tightly prescribed understandings of what success looks like. In their place are lived experiences of leadership in a faith community or other ministry setting that offer opportunities for learning. There are open-ended goals and objectives that the one engaged in Supervised Ministry is to self-identify and apply to their own situation and learning context, and there is an invitation to identify for themselves what ministerial formation and growth toward competency will look like in their learning environment.

My understanding of the sort of work done in Supervised Ministry leads me to believe that the learning that happens in such experiences is situated firmly in the constructivist approach to education. This model of education asserts that

> the learner is actively constructing knowledge rather than passively taking in information. Learners come to the educational setting with many different experiences, ideas, and approaches to learning. Learners do not *acquire* knowledge that is transmitted to them; rather, they *construct* knowledge through their intellectual activity and make it their own.[2]

Perhaps you participated in such learning opportunities while in traditional classroom settings in higher education. But now that you are in a setting of Supervised Ministry, it is the prime focus for your learning. You will be encouraged, and even required, to take an even more active role in your learning. The Supervised Ministry learning experience requires you to engage in an action-reflection-action model of education that invites you to use your own lived experience as the text to be studied and reflected on. It is your own ministry that offers up concepts to wrestle with and theories to integrate into further learning.

Through practicing ministry, learning and refining the skills needed to lead communities of faith in their life together, exercising other kinds of ministerial leadership, and reflecting theologically on your own vocational formation, you are asked to actively construct your own knowledge, bringing meaning to what might otherwise be seen as disparate actions and data. Those facilitating such learning opportunities for you understand that you are, as Jack Mezirow asserts in his work on transformational learning theories, "old enough to be held responsible for [your] acts to acquire or enhance [your] understandings, skills, and dispositions."[3] This kind of learning opportunity is yours to develop and to take advantage of, should you choose to fully embrace the challenge.

True learning will not occur unless or until you engage in the important task of critical reflection. Meaning will be elusive, missing, or at best only partially formed without times for intentional theological reflection. As Laura Foote explains, "critical reflection involves evaluating assumptions, beliefs, attitudes, practices, and tacit knowledge; in other words, that which has previously been taken for granted."[4] No doubt, learning will happen as you go about the activities and practices of your Supervised Ministry, but the true work of integration and formation cannot happen without meaningful periods of reflection.

This sort of reflection does not come easily. Ann Stanton, in her work on transformative learning, observes that "most adults simply have not developed their capacities for articulating and criticizing the underlying assumptions of their own thinking, nor do they analyze the thinking of others in this way."[5] Critical reflection is not an activity that we are invited to engage in with any regularity throughout our formative years, and it is a concept that remains fairly elusive to us as we come to educational opportunities in our adult years.

Because this is the case, reflection needs to be structured in ways that encourage you, the learner, to go below the surface when examining your thoughts and actions. Only then will underlying motives and biases become clear. Only then will your lived meaning-making system be held up next to the one you share publicly—making clear where those two coincide and where they differ or even contradict each other!

Accountability partners are also important for critical reflection. These partners come in many different forms—individually (through activities like journaling) and with supervisor-mentors, lay committees, cohorts of learners in other Supervised Ministry settings, and institutional staff and faculty. By inviting conversation partners into your reflective practice, you will have more opportunities to delve deeply into the material of your lived experience and gain insights that otherwise might have eluded you. Through these conversations, with yourself and with others, you are given the opportunity to sit with and give deliberate attention to the ever-looming question of meaning.

Seeking answers to the question "What does it all mean?" is central to being human, according to Mezirow, who asserts that "a defining condition of being human is our urgent need to understand and order the meaning of our experience, to integrate it with what we know to avoid the threat of chaos."[6] This threat of chaos seems very real because of the sheer amount of data that our lives present us with. Until that data is brought together as a whole, it remains a hulking menace that could cave in on us at any moment.

THE POWER OF STORY

This is where stories can play a crucial role. As Donald Polkinghorne explains, "narrative is a meaning structure that organizes events and human action into a whole, thereby attributing significance to individual actions and events according to their effect on the whole."[7] Such structure provides an antidote to chaos. It can bring coherence and tame the beast that threatens to overwhelm us. Structure provides the meaning we humans crave. It organizes the pieces of our lives through stories—both ours and those of others—bringing all the pieces together in a meaningful whole.

Stories are as close to us as is our breath. Stories surround us from our births and accompany us until our deaths. Many of us feel at peace with leaving this corporeal world when we know that stories of our lives and their worth will continue on after we are no longer here to share them ourselves. Rossiter and Clark, in surveying the literature on narrative theory, note major themes in what is meant by this overarching idea of "meaning." They note that various authors have proposed that "meaning has to do with values and beliefs . . . , with context . . . , [and] with interpretation," concluding that "to make meaning narratively means that we understand the raw material of our existence in a story-like form."[8]

We can all probably remember being in the presence of a masterful storyteller, someone who not only was able to tell the facts of an event or experience but who made us feel like we were right there with them, experiencing it for ourselves. We can most likely just as readily recall someone who struggled to get their story across. The details were too many, and the wrangling of them seemed rough. We might have gotten the sense of what the speaker was trying to convey, but we were not swept up into the experience itself.

While stories are all around us and are a steady part of our daily diet, it doesn't mean that they are always easy for us to use. Polkinghorne acknowledges this when he posits that "the process of seeing human actions as meaningful sequences of events linked together in a causal chain requires cognitive skills, judgement, and the application of previous experiences. When the story-making process is successful, it provides a coherent and plausible account of how and why something has happened."[9] The process doesn't always work well. It takes practice. Periods of theological reflection afford one the opportunity for such practice at storytelling in a supportive environment where failure is allowed and even encouraged.

It might seem weird to think about failing at storytelling, but it happens with great regularity. It can occur when we start down the path of telling a story only to find that it doesn't adequately account for all the data we are trying to make sense of. Storytelling necessarily highlights some points and minimizes or discards others in order for the whole to have meaning. We don't always get that right the first time around. Perhaps we leave out something that we later realize is important to the overall story we are trying to tell. Or, perhaps we realize that we are giving too much weight to a thread of the story that really isn't as important as we are making it seem.

CURATING OUR STORY

The process of selecting, ordering, and weighing the events and data of our lives can be a positive experience. "Life narratives are retrospective, always in process, unfolding. [This] . . . can be 'empowering.' . . . [We] do have some choice as to how we interpret [the data]."[10] We may find that on one occasion in one context, we take the raw data of our lives and tell the story in one way, while on another occasion in another context, we curate our story in a very different way. The people who surround us and the situations we are in while we are telling this story, whether to others or only to ourselves, influence how the story develops.

While the process of meaning making through story can often be empowering, as noted above, it can also be disempowering. When the stories we hear around us are not in harmony with the story we are telling ourselves, or when our stories are not heard or valued, the process can be harmful. Foote reminds us, "Identity construction is rooted in the stories humans believe about themselves. Change the story, change the human's identity."[11] This can be either helpful or detrimental depending on the agency one is given in the process. There are times when we come to understand that the story we are telling is not the truth and has been holding us or others back in our growth. In such cases, it is good to revise the story so that new growth can happen.

The process of storytelling can also be detrimental to people when whole stories are omitted or reinterpreted in ways incongruent with the actual facts as they occurred. Polkinghorne warns us of this potential when he writes, "Narrative can retrospectively alter the meaning of events after the final outcome is known."[12] We in the United States of America are slowly coming to a greater awareness of this very fact as indigenous peoples, African Americans, and other marginalized groups bring to light their own stories that have not been included in the cultural storytelling of our collective history as a nation.

It is important to remember this potential for great harm as we embark on the process of meaning making through storytelling. Only when we do so will we be able to avoid engaging in storytelling that harms ourselves and others. The hope for people of faith should be that all are able to see their own individual stories reflected within the larger stories told in the culture at large. A positive benefit will come from this, as Polkinghorne explains: "Narrative enrichment occurs when one retrospectively revises, selects, and orders past details in such a way as to create a self-narrative that is coherent and satisfying and that will serve as a justification for one's present condition and situation. The retrospective revision needs to conclude and coincide with the known present."[13]

THEOLOGICAL REFLECTION AND LEARNING ENVIRONMENTS

Times of intentional theological reflection, individually and with conversation partners, are vital for allowing you in the Supervised Ministry experience to contemplate the stories that you are telling to see if they are empowering or disempowering, inclusive of all voices or leaving out voices that are critical to the narrative of the whole community. When you engage in this type of intentional reflection, it "creates the possibility for critique, for the questioning of underlying assumptions, of power relations, of whose interests are served by a particular narrative and whose interests are being exploited."[14]

This critique may be uncomfortable for you because it often exposes blind spots in your worldview. In such situations, you will need help to get out of your own situatedness in order to gain a more expansive view. Mezirow helpfully speaks to the knowledge gaps that can exist and how they might be addressed. In his study of transformational learning, he writes, "Imagination is central to understanding the unknown; it is the way we examine alternative interpretations of our experience by 'trying on' another's point of view."[15] Sometimes you might be able to make leaps of imagination on your own, leaps that will help you to bridge such gaps. But often you will need help finding ways to expand your thinking in order to get closer to the experience of others unfamiliar to yourself.

The learning environment is critical for ensuring that learning in such situations is effective. Maria Kish lays out what she believes is helpful to consider when creating learning spaces in which storytelling is a major component. According to Kish, "The learning environment best suited for adults is supportive, focuses on course goals and individual goals of the adult learner, promotes active learning, and considers learning activities that assist adults in transferring their learning to their own situations, and one that provides flexibility for the adults' learning needs."[16]

These are exactly the types of settings that Supervised Ministry can afford you as a learner. Sites and supervisor-mentors come to these programs ready to welcome those who are interested in engaging in active learning and in being formed for future ministry. They are eager to provide environments in which you can try out different ideas and practices, welcoming failure as a vital learning opportunity, not a dreaded foe. And they, along with your cohort, provide regular opportunities for asking questions and offering feedback with the intent of helping you to integrate what you are experiencing so that you can set patterns for future ministry.

There are three major ways in which our stories are incorporated into the learning that happens in a Supervised Ministry experience. They occur through regular check-ins where stories of varying lengths are shared and reflected on, through the sharing of critical incident reports or verbatims that seek to encapsulate a specific encounter for feedback and learning, and through the process of regular formal evaluation.

First, let's consider regular check-ins. These can happen spontaneously following an event or encounter, but more often they occur at a regularly scheduled time set aside for being together—a period meant for intentional reflection. The stories that are shared in these gatherings may be a quick recap to set the intentions for reflections that will follow, or they may be a more in-depth retelling of events with the aim of giving a thorough picture of how you experienced the event or encounter.

In these situations, you are engaging in storytelling as McDrury understands it: "a uniquely human experience that enables us to convey, through the language of words, aspects of ourselves and others, and the worlds, real or imagined, that we inhabit."[17] In telling your story, you are inviting the listener into the world as you experienced it. You invite the other to view a situation through your eyes and to experience the event or encounter in the way in which you yourself did. Most often, you will only be able to hear feedback or suggestions about how to improve your actions and reactions when you feel that the other has truly entered into the space of deep listening and experiencing your story. Only then will you be able to truly grow from the reflections that are offered in response.

A second way that stories are often used in Supervised Ministry settings is through critical incident reports or verbatims. These are a regular part of learning that happens in the Clinical Pastoral Education units that mostly take place in hospital settings. They can be used effectively in other Supervised Ministry settings as well.

This exercise invites you to choose an encounter or practice of ministry on which you would like to reflect intentionally. You then write up a brief but thorough report of the encounter, paying careful attention to relaying the actual events as accurately as possible. You should include in the report conversations, emotions, and theological issues that arose during the encounter, including enough detail to give those reading it a good sense of what occurred but not drowning them in minutiae.

The main goal of this exercise is to get different perspectives on the encounter in order to identify what were the main needs of the encounter, to see if they were adequately addressed in the interaction, and to evaluate how the encounter could have gone differently or been more helpful to all involved. Those who meet with you after reading such reports ask clarifying questions, offer reflections on what they see happening in the scenario, and open up other ways of understanding what might have been happening in the encounter. All of this will allow you to consider new or different ways to approach similar situations in the future.

The third major way that storytelling is employed in Supervised Ministry experiences comes through periods of formal evaluation. Evaluation forms used by different institutions vary widely, but all ask you and your supervisor-mentor (and typically a committee of members from the community as well) to reflect on past experience in the learning site in order to measure the amount of growth that has occurred within a specific time period. Evaluators are asked to measure growth toward meeting the learning goals of both you and the institution. Often evaluation forms will ask for short paragraphs that give examples of how learning has or has not happened or to explain how it is anticipated it will happen in the future. Filling out the forms gives each of the parties the opportunity to tell stories from their own perspective about the ministry in which you are engaged. When taken together, the forms bring these stories together to give a more wholistic view of the ministry that you are providing.

While the activity of completing the forms is an important one, it is incomplete until you and the other evaluators have discussed together what each has written. By retelling and reinterpreting the stories the evaluation forms contain, you are invited into a space where substantial insights and growth can occur. As Rossiter and Clark explain, "Autobiographical writing . . . requires reflection on our lived experience and leads adult learners to heightened insight into their own learning and development."[18] This will happen most especially for you, but it will also happen for all who are involved in the evaluative writing exercise.

In all three of these ways of using stories in experiences of Supervised Ministry, you are engaging in storytelling in the hope that reflecting on past experience will guide future action. Whether you have identified actions and thoughts that will be helpful for future ministry or actions or those that were not as helpful and should be amended or avoided in future ministry, the act of reflecting through storytelling helps to set future patterns.

Sharing stories within cohort settings brings additional benefits. When you hear the stories of others, these "stories can function as a substitute for direct experience . . . [and] help [you] to gain experience vicariously."[19] In a cohort, you and your fellow learners will hear about ministry that is happening in different settings and about learning that you and your colleagues are engaged in. Through this process each is able to glean ideas for their own future ministry.

In Supervised Ministry experiences, the supervisor-mentor, lay committee, and the community at large take on the role of the educator for you. As such, they are charged with playing the three distinct but interrelated educator roles that Mezirow has identified:

> First . . . to assist learners in becoming aware of their psychological preferences.
> Second . . . in encouraging critical questioning of psychological habits of mind and supporting the differentiation of the individual from the collective.
> [And] third . . . to help create learning experiences that involve learners of different predispositions in that process.[20]

Of course, the Supervised Ministry sites are not alone in this work. Academic faculty and staff from your institution are there to provide training and support for the site as well as to continue working directly with you in facilitating theological reflection and integration, individually and within your cohort.

The question remains: What does it all mean?

Telling and retelling our stories, shaping and reshaping our reality and the worlds we live in, naming the lived experiences and bringing them to light in new and different ways helps us get ever closer to finding answers that satisfy this question. Having conversation partners who listen to our stories and engage in meaningful reflection with us adds to the richness and complexity that our stories bring to the learning process.

QUESTIONS FOR REFLECTION

1. Can you think of a time when you were able to tell a story effectively to an audience (small or large)? Can you also think of a time when you were not so effective in your storytelling effort? What made the difference in those experiences?
2. When have you been invited to bring your stories into a learning experience? How did sharing your stories enhance your learning in those situations?
3. Have you witnessed or experienced a time when storytelling harmed you or others? Why was it harmful? How could it have been done differently to avoid that outcome?

SUGGESTED READING

Mark C. Carnes, *Minds on Fire: How Role-Immersion Games Transform College* (Cambridge, MA: Harvard University Press, 2014).

Amy E. Spaulding, *The Art of Storytelling: Telling Truths through Telling Stories* (Lanham, MD: Rowman & Littlefield, 2011).

Chapter Six

Learning the Practice of Story Sharing in Community

Erik Samuelson

> Tell a story about a time when you learned something important about yourself and ministry through the telling of stories.

On a Friday morning in November we gathered, as we did each Friday, in the third classroom from the end of the hall. The chairs had been arranged in a circle around a low table covered in a blue, slightly reflective fabric on which several objects sat: a pinecone, a candle, a small icon of Saint Francis, a singing bowl, and a cross. With lights dimmed and meditative music playing in the background, about a dozen first-year college students slowly came in and found their places. When the last straggler appeared (clearly fresh from their bunkbed), the students were welcomed, the singing bowl rung three times, and we set about the first task of the day: a story-telling spiritual practice called holy listening.

"To 'listen' another's soul into a condition of disclosure and discovery may be almost the greatest service that any human being ever performs for another," I reminded them, quoting Douglass Steere. "So when you listen to your partner's story this morning, give them your full attention, listen deeply from your heart, and act as if you have all the time in the world (though you will only have two minutes!)." Then I gave them the prompt of the day: "Tell a story about a time when you overcame something that you thought you couldn't." After two minutes of silent reflection, I invited the students to find a partner—preferably someone they hadn't engaged with before. I watched with great interest (as I always did) as the students self-selected into pairs. On this morning I was surprised to see two particular students lock eyes with one another and realize that they were the last unpaired pair in the room.

I'm pretty sure I'd never seen these two students ever say a single word to one another, as they came from nearly entirely different worlds. She had grown up in a very monocultural community not far from the gathering places of neo-Nazi groups, where she was part of the majority white culture and didn't have much experience with people of color until coming to college. He, in stark contrast, was from an inner-city high school where no ethnic group held a majority and as a young black man had experienced firsthand the impacts of generational poverty and racism. If you set out to pick two students who had nearly nothing in common, these would be your two. And so I watched (without looking like I was watching) as they settled in and engaged this holy listening practice: listening for two minutes without comment as their partner spoke their truth into the room and then trading roles with the first speaking while the other listened. As he was telling his story, suddenly her face changed—it softened, and she leaned in as she listened. When it came time for her to tell her story she was like a different person, and you could see the energy being generated between them. Clearly something significant had happened.

As the students gathered back together to debrief the experience, I asked them, "How was that for you?" and these two were the first to speak. In two minutes of telling and listening to each other's stories, they had come to a shocking conclusion: though they seemed as different as can be, in their stories they discovered they shared a point of pain, a common struggle, a similar obstacle overcome—something they likely would never have discovered about the other if they hadn't had this conversation that morning. And from that moment on, they became the best of friends—overcoming all manner of cultural, socioeconomic, and racial differences through the simple sharing of their stories with one another. And something shifted in the whole group that day. They all were drawn closer into relationship with each other. As they continued week after week to share stories with one another, they were led into increasingly deep reflection as the year went on. They were not just engaging the content of the course but also learning experientially how to engage cross-culturally, how use story to integrate what they were experiencing into the curriculum of their lives and, perhaps most importantly, how to make meaning in community.

It was nearly a decade ago that I was called to be the campus pastor of a small, mainline Christian college in the Pacific Northwest, where I oversaw the worship, care, and spiritual life of an incredibly diverse student body. Along with that position came a second: director of vocational and spiritual formation. It was in the second role that I facilitated this first-year course called Vocation and Formation that put 10–12 first-year students in small groups weekly with a faculty instructor/mentor for reflection, vocational exploration, and spiritual practices. The course curriculum I inherited had been designed for a student population that no longer reflected our community: the deeply involved youth-group president (usually white), this-denomination-Christian students who were now a minority on a campus with students of many races from many different spiritual traditions (including none of the above). It was only a matter of weeks before I realized that the course needed a major overhaul to respond to the needs and life experience of these students, and so my own experiential learning came through experimenting with the structure and content of the course itself—trying out different modes and practices to see what resonated and with whom and reflecting on and refining the material and teaching approach along the way.

As it turned out, this experimental-experiential learning mode was exactly what allowed these students to connect with the content and with one another. In addition to the holy listening storytelling practice (which we did each week), over the course of the year our groups experienced a whole range of Christian spiritual practices. "The only way to learn a spiritual practice," I would tell them, "is to practice. And remember, not everything will work for everyone. So, you may hate this—but we'll talk about it afterwards and next week we'll be on to something else." The freedom to explore, to draw in their previous experience, and to try on new ways of engaging created a powerful learning environment. The practice of action-reflection with their peers (who, it turns out, were struggling with similar things) became a community-building experience. It impacted the classroom, and over the course of several years we recognized a story-sharing culture shift happening across the college as students were listening and learning from one another. But, to my surprise, the most profound impact of this course was not on the students who were enrolled. No, the deepest transformation I witnessed was among the faculty who were facilitating these groups—something they never expected.

It took an entire year before I could convince our new academic dean to lead a vocation and formation group. After my first "no," I recruited my other instructors to bombard him with stories from their groups—of getting to know the students in a new way, of hearing amazing stories of what these students bring from their lives and experiences, of witnessing powerful transformation and unexpected connections like the story I just relayed. It was a wonderful and diverse group of instructors—our dean of students, who had grown up the child of missionaries, a creative writing professor who had considered seminary, a candidate for the Lutheran Deaconess Community, a missionary on her final assignment after more than 40 years overseas, and others with similarly interesting backgrounds. They had really great stories from their experiences leading these groups, and somehow we eventually wore our dean down, and he agreed to facilitate a group. It was only much later that I learned that, while his "I'm too busy" rationale was certainly true, his actual hesitation was in not feeling competent to teach in this way. He was an academic, used to the rigor and structure of presenting and evaluating information. Though a person of deep faith, he confessed that he didn't feel comfortable bringing his own story and practice into the classroom or know how to invite students into such an open-ended experience and reflection. And he wasn't alone; across the board I heard the instructors relay similar concerns and struggles.

The dean shared this one Friday morning in the instructors' gathering, which we always held an hour before the student groups met—a community of practice for us professors learning together how to teach experientially and engage with our incredibly diverse student body. We also would practice together, experientially learning some spiritual practice we were going to teach our students, debriefing our session from the week before, and often bringing a teaching challenge we were facing, be it from this course or another. We had built enough trust among that group of instructors (who, it turns out again, were struggling with similar things) for the usually stalwart academics, the lifelong teachers of spiritualty, and even me—a pastor who ought to know how to do such things—to admit that often we felt in over our heads, that we struggled to connect to our students, that a particular practice or another was hard to teach because we didn't find it engaging ourselves.

I was privileged in that community to witness (and participate in) the deep transformation of this community of teachers, who little by little were developing into true spiritual elders—practitioners of deep theological and vocational reflection who embodied what they sought to teach. We all were challenged in ways we never could have imagined, but to a person we look back on those experiences as a powerful and transformative time that deeply impacted our teaching, our spirituality, and our own sense of vocation. I don't know how else we could have learned the things we learned (and then taught) except by experiencing and reflecting on our experience and by sharing stories with one another as we constructed shared meaning in community. My own work and ministry were deeply transformed as I saw firsthand the power of story, of speaking and listening to one we consider "other," and learned the art of curating space for these transformative experiences to emerge. And it all started with the words: "Tell a story about a time when..."

Chapter Seven

We Refuse to Be Enemies

Being Defined and Connected in Israel and Palestine

Marijke Strong

Just across the road from the old city of Jerusalem, the Golden Walls Hotel looms up like an ancient Middle Eastern fortress. In a hot, bustling neighborhood with hundreds of vendors shouting for attention, the hotel sits silently on the street corner, its stone walls cool to the touch. It was in the sub-basement of the Golden Walls Hotel that I learned a new way of seeing. I was with a small group on a two-week trip to Israel/Palestine. We had come to offer an arts camp for children in the West Bank, to study the holy sites, and to learn about the Israeli-Palestinian conflict.

The week before, our group had led a pilot project camp for children in Beit Sahour, a town just outside of Bethlehem. The camp week culminated in a collaborative mural made with the children titled "The Peaceable Kingdom." Realizing our own ignorance, we had tentatively talked with the kids throughout that week about their dreams for a future of peace, when "the wolf will live with the lamb . . . and a little child will lead them." And the children truly became our teachers. We had come to Israel and Palestine hoping to help these kids living under occupation find space to imagine peace, but actually it was the children who led us that week, turning the tables on us by showing us the greatest wisdom, calmest hope, deepest forgiveness, and warmest hospitality we had ever seen.

All this was still fresh in our minds when we returned to the Golden Walls Hotel and descended into the sub-basement. Outside we could hear the muffled sounds of traffic, shouts of passersby, and the call of the muezzin from a nearby mosque. It was a blazing hot day. Inside the room was quieter and cooler but still stuffy. It smelled, our guide liked to say, like *life*. We drew the patterned hotel chairs into a circle and made two extra spaces for the men who were there to speak to us.

I knew very little about Rami and Bassam, other than that one was a Palestinian and one was an Israeli, they had both experienced violent conflict for most of their lives, and they were speakers for a group called Parents' Circle/Family Forum. I did not know that what they would say in the next hour would change my life and would continue to inspire and challenge me spiritually for years to come.

They sat next to each other, and it was clear from the start that they had a deep love and respect for each other. Rami began by putting his arm around Bassam with a grin, saying, "My name is Rami Elhanan. I am a Jew. I am an Israeli. Before anything else, I am a human being. This Palestinian is my dear brother. In many ways he is one of the closest people to me on earth. What makes us so close is the price we both have paid as an outcome of this ongoing conflict between our two nations."

Bassam's eyes looked down during Rami's speech, but at this point he raised them and we saw the quiet strength in his gaze. "My name is Bassam Aramim. I am a Palestinian. I spent seven years in an Israeli jail for a mistake I made when I was 12. And I am proud to call this ex-enemy, this man, my brother. Because we are fighting together, we are struggling together, for peace."

They went on to tell their personal stories of horror, hatred, and loss. Rami described his daughter, Smadar. She was, in his words, a beautiful, amazing, vivid, sparkling little girl. He said everyone called her The Princess. The family lived a good life in a house in Jerusalem: Rami, his wife (a professor at the university), their three boys, and The Princess. It seemed like the perfect existence. But then on September 4, 1997, the bubble they were living in was blown up by two Palestinian suicide bombers who exploded themselves in Ben Yehuda street, killing five people, including three young girls. One of them was 14-year-old Smadar.

Bassam told the story of his daughter, Abir. On January 16, 2007, in front of her grade school, an Israeli police officer shot her in the back of the head from a distance of 15–20 meters. She died several hours later. She was 10 years old.

The men spoke of their inconsolable grief, their shock, their anger, their depression, their hatred . . . and finally their desire for healing and peace. It was that desire that brought them to Parents' Circle, an organization committed to bringing grieving Palestinians and Israelis together for reconciliation.

Rami admitted with shame that until he entered the organization at the age of 47, he had never looked at a Palestinian as a human being. Now he says, "Our blood is exactly the same color. Our pain is exactly the same pain. Our tears are exactly the same bitterness. And if we, who paid the highest price possible, can talk to each other, then anyone can, and anyone should.

We can break once and for all the endless cycle of violence and revenge. The only way to do it is simply by talking to each other. It will not stop until we talk. We do not ask you to be pro-Israeli or pro-Palestinian. We demand of you to be pro-peace."

Our group was profoundly impacted by Rami and Bassam. We spoke about them, their stories, and their challenge for days to come. But the learning did not end there. The next week, we visited Tent of Nations, a Palestinian organic farm that is frequently threatened and sometimes even bulldozed by Israeli soldiers because of its prime location for Israeli settlements. The Nassar family, owners of the farm, had also committed themselves to healing and peace. They had established a peace camp for Palestinian and Israeli students to come together, and they hosted groups like ours for discussions about reconciliation.

When we drove onto the farm property, we were greeted at the end of the dusty lane by a large rock with the words "WE REFUSE TO BE ENEMIES" written in three languages. Daoud Nassar spoke with us at length, ending his speech with the words, "We are determined to stay. But we are also determined that whatever violence we experience here at the hands of others we will turn to good, to peace."

All of this undid me. Because, interspersed with these experiences of wise children, embattled farmers, and reconciled enemies, we were also touring the biblical holy sites and visiting churches and mosques that had been fought over, where people had been shot dead in the name of God. It made me question everything I thought I knew about a God of restorative justice and the church as God's instrument for peace. I found myself confused and angry but also excited.

I was confused in my growing realization that the ancient holy sites inspired me less than the stories of real people we were meeting who were working for peace in times of war. To be sure, the holy sites were historically fascinating, but I was realizing that I cared less about where Jesus walked in the past than I cared about where he was walking now. Or, more to the point, with whom he was walking now.

I was also angry because I was sensing how ineffective the North American church was in engaging with issues of injustice like the ones I was seeing right in front of me. I felt helpless, with my Bible in hand, as I surveyed the Nassars' farm and heard their tale of oppression and hope. What was a North American pastor to do? And how was it possible that I had been blind to this situation for so long? I was angry at the church and at myself.

But I was also excited. I felt my energy rising as I saw my own inner tensions confronted by the people of Israel and Palestine and felt the Spirit's invitation into a new way of being.

The reality was that I had gone into that trip with a boatload of my own tension. To start, I had a chip on my shoulder about "mission trips." I had experienced a mission trip a decade earlier that had had a distinctly colonial feel to it. Although the people on that trip went into it with the best of intentions, our work project had ended up feeling a bit charitable and one-sided. It did not foster reciprocal relationship and mutual learning with our hosts. Of course, one-sided relief is sometimes necessary, especially in emergency situations. But my experience of that earlier mission trip, compounded by stories I had heard from friends about similar trips, led me to think that the mission trip model too often lent itself to an imbalanced relationship between the "haves" and the "have nots" at the expense of a respectful mutuality.

I was also in a state of emotional and spiritual fatigue; I was about two years into my first charge as a workaholic local church pastor in a denomination that was fighting about human sexuality, and the fight was turning ugly. When I arrived in Jerusalem, I found myself questioning the institutional church in general: feeling cynical about mission trips, fatigued with local church ministry, and seriously grieved about the dysfunction in my denomination. But as it turned out, the people of Israel and Palestine were about to teach me a new way of seeing the world and of understanding myself. The key, I think, was their emotional maturity.

Their stories underscored one of the simplest definitions of emotional maturity: the ability to be both defined and connected.

Being defined in relationships has two parts. First, we define ourselves when we take a position. In other words, when we say (with our words and our actions), "This is what I think and believe, this is what I want, this is what I am doing, this is where I stand." Second, being defined in relationships means that we allow others to define themselves by taking a position. We make room for them to say (with their words and their actions) what they think, believe, want, and will do, and where they stand, even if their position is different from our own.

Being connected to others means we can stay in relationship with them at a level of intensity appropriate to the relationship without taking our self away from them or giving up self to them. We are appropriately connected when we care for them without taking care of them, when we are responsible to them without being responsible for them, and when we stay in one-to-one contact with them even in the face of conflict and emotional tension.

The people of Israel/Palestine who are working for peace are the best examples I have ever seen of being both defined and connected in the midst of an impossible, violent conflict. Despite suffering unimaginable pain at one another's hands, I see them choosing to say who they are, to tell their stories of horror and joy, to stay where they live, to speak courageously about what they think ... and at the same time they are choosing to see their enemies as human beings, to move toward one another in their differences, to listen, to talk, and to work together for the healing they dream might one day bring their two nations together.

This level of emotional maturity was completely new to me, and it confronted all my internal tensions head-on.

When our hosts at the art camp invited me into their homes to share their stories and to listen to my own story with deep interest, they showed me how to make a "mission trip" an experience of reciprocity, mutuality, and shared learning. Although I was sincerely asked to offer my own gifts, I found myself more often taking the posture of a student.

When our guides to the holy sites explained the realities of war by bringing us through burned-out cities and into mosques riddled with bullet holes, they showed me how to be a pastor without fusing to my congregation. I saw that it was possible both to care for someone and to challenge them, without taking responsibility for their emotions. It was my emotional fusion to my congregation back home that had caused me to overfunction for them, to the point of burnout. In Israel and Palestine, I found myself guided, taught, and cared for by people who could let me sit with those deeper feelings for a while in order to learn from them.

When an oppressed farmer boldly spoke out of his personal identity and stated his political positions in the face of violent opposition, and when he sought at the same time to find peace with his enemies, he showed me that my own conflicts were reconcilable if I could learn to move toward the other in love.

When I consider the people of Israel and Palestine, I am both embarrassed and inspired by their example. They teach me to see my own so-called intractable problems in a different light. And I think, "If these people can learn to love in such an impossible situation, surely I can do it too." As Rami said, "If we who paid the highest price possible can talk to each other, then anyone can, and anyone should." So, when I want to give up on the institutional church because of its dysfunctions and divisions, when I want to throw in the towel on the fatigues of local ministry, when I want to complain because being emotionally mature is such hard work, I remember Rami and Bassam—their powerful determination to be defined and connected in the midst of conflict—and I try again.

Chapter Eight

My Story, God's Call

Erika Tobin Bergh

I love my mother. I really do. And I love the work that she does, but I also have always wanted to be my own person and go my own way. My mother is an Evangelical Lutheran Church in America deacon and the director of children's ministries at Gloria Dei Lutheran Church in Olympia, Washington. She works with people ages birth through death, but her heart, her passion, and her focus is on ages birth through sixth grade. I grew up within the role of a pastor's kid without a pastor for a parent. I was always at church, always knowing the answers to questions in Sunday school, and everyone knew who I was even if I didn't know who they were.

Our dinner table conversations often revolved around new curriculum my mom was writing for Sunday school a few months out or about new ideas for vacation Bible school curriculum. We listened to musicals and kids' choir songs in the car as she drove us to and from school. And I always knew where Pastors Phil and Kurt hid their candy stashes. Life constantly revolved around church, and I loved it! It meant I had an identity, an extended family, and a second home.

Fast-forward a decade to college-aged Erika. I'm taking more seriously the question "What do you want to be when you grow up?" I was torn between high school choir director, spiritual director, youth director, pastor, occupational therapist, college religion professor, librarian, and Crayola coloring book tester. I didn't even consider working with kids younger than high school age. At this point it wasn't because of a named desire to not go down the same career path as my mom; it was simply because I wanted to wrestle with the big questions in life, and I didn't know how to do that with younger kids.

But now, fast-forward again, this time about eight years. Seminarian Erika is on internship, serving at a congregation in Arizona that was intentionally exploring what cross-generational ministry looked like in their context. One of my goals for the internship was to narrow down what I felt called to: hospital chaplaincy or parish ministry. A call to youth ministry was in the back of my mind, but it was not an option I was seriously considering. So, upon beginning my internship, I expressed a desire to *not* work closely with the kids and youth programs (although I would still help and be involved as needed). I wanted to focus more on ministry with adults and the elderly. I passed it off to myself as a need to grow in an area I had less experience in. Although this was very true, it was not the deeper (and therefore more accurate) reason.

I had grown up seeing the behind-the-scenes preparations for children's ministry while also growing up in those ministries as a participant. I had volunteered with vacation Bible school programs and in that way helped create children's ministry. I had served as a counselor and then dean of students at Lutheran Summer Music Academy and Festival and helped kids for four summers explore God, music, and community for four weeks of their summer break. I had served on my synod's Lutheran Youth Organization board and put on middle and high school retreats and service events around the synod. And I had witnessed and been a part of a birth to twelfth-grade Sunday school program that grew from 30 to 150 kids. I considered myself to have enough experience with children's and youth ministries to be able to step back and focus on other age groups that I was less experienced with while I was on internship.

And yet, I found myself most happy while exploring Bible stories and praying with the church's day care kids during weekly chapel. I found myself most happy during the children's sermons each Sunday. And I found myself most happy when talking with five-year-olds about how they think Jesus karate chops down doors to get to us. I couldn't help noticing that I was most happy when interacting with kids. I felt the pull toward kids and youth, and yet I ignored it. I didn't bring it up during supervisory sessions with my supervising pastor, Pastor Mark. I didn't write about it in my journal. I didn't pray about it. I just ignored it and kept focusing on learning more about adult Bible studies and other adult-centered ministries.

Until January.

I'm not sure what changed six months into my internship during the month of January, but something shifted. I found myself unable to sleep one night, and I had the overwhelming sense of "I am about to explode if I don't say this out loud." But even then, fear kept me from saying it to the dark, empty room that enveloped me. Fear kept me from saying it to God, the only other entity listening to my sobs as I desperately tried not to explode but also tried not to name the thought that was pounding around in my head. I was too afraid. I was afraid that as a woman I would get pigeonholed into children's ministry and never be able to do anything else if I ever wanted to. I was afraid that I wouldn't be able to be myself, that I'd just be a mini version of my mom. I was afraid that I would be viewed as simply living into, and perpetuating, the stereotype that women are the ones who work with kids and men work with the adults. And I was afraid, if I named the thought in my head, that I wouldn't be able to ever work with older people as well.

Eventually, around 4:00 a.m., a source of hope appeared within me: I could tell my supervisor-mentor. Pastor Mark would be able to talk this through with me. He could help me figure out this fear, this thought, and this threat of exploding. But it was 4:00 a.m. He couldn't help me then. He was asleep. So, I told myself to wait till 6:00 a.m. to text him, and in the meantime, I'd give in and name it to myself and to God.

"I want to work with kids. I want to work with youth."

Such simple sentences. Yet the emotion that poured out from me while I lay in bed in that dark, empty room was beyond overwhelming. Relief, as well as fear, poured out of me upon uttering those words in the direction of the spinning ceiling fan. But the relief was stronger than the fear. By giving in to the thought pounding around in my head, I somewhat staved off the feeling of exploding, and the anxiety created by the fears was lessened as well. Enough pressure had been released that I was able to calm down, but now I had to wait till Pastor Mark could meet with me.

The waiting was agony, but finally our agreed-upon meeting time came. I walked into his office, sat down in a chair across from him at his desk, and started with some teary-eyed preamble that I no longer remember the contents of. I eventually got to the telling of the story of my night, my fears, and the thought in my head: "I want to work with kids. I want to work with youth." As I choked out the story, my body was wracked with tears of relief at getting this thought, this call, this need named out loud to another human being—a human being specially placed by God in my life for the exact purpose of doing this kind of discovery and reflection. As I named my fears to him, his eyes watered with tears of his own, and he nodded in contemplation. Once my stream of words and tears had slowed, Pastor Mark began the process of unpacking all that had been delivered in that space.

He shared his gratitude for my sharing of this epiphany. He expressed similarly noticing my joy when around kids that wasn't quite as prevalent around people of older ages (although I still exuded joy). And then he arrived at my fears. He took them one by one and carefully held them and acknowledged them while offering me ways to think of them without letting them hold me back from acting on my now-named desire to work with kids and youth. He helped me think through ways that I could avoid being pigeonholed within children's and youth ministry while being a woman who deeply enjoys interacting with kids and God at the same time. He helped me think through how in the grand scheme of things it wouldn't matter if I appeared to be perpetuating a stereotype; I was following a calling! He helped me think through ways I wouldn't be a mini version of my mom while still holding her work and her creativity in admiration and inspiration. And he helped me think through ways I could still work with people of older ages at the same time as I work with kids and youth. As Pastor Mark talked through each of my fears, the anxiety within me lessened further, and the relief was increasingly profound.

We ended the supervisory session in prayer, deep breaths, and grateful silence. As I left his office, I couldn't help but notice how much lighter I felt. No matter how many times my counselors told me over the years, "Erika, don't bottle things up and keep them inside you. Get them out. Tell someone!" somehow that lesson was still hard to remember until that day. After telling my story to Pastor Mark, I shared it with my internship lay committee. Profuse affirmations flowed my way from the committee along with abundant support of my newly named sense of calling and purpose. As the weeks went on from that January epiphany, members of my internship church and friends around town commented on how they noticed a change in me: my steps seemed to have more pep in them, the light in my eyes was brighter, and I appeared freer and more confident in my interactions with people of all ages.

To have those observations named helped me understand the power of sharing my story in the context of a supervisory and mentoring relationship. Being vulnerable, sharing my inner thoughts on how I am doing in response to lived experience and what I am feeling drawn toward, provided me with valuable learning I could never have received in a classroom. I don't know what would have happened had I not shared my story with Pastor Mark, but I know it was becoming increasingly impossible not to. And still to this day, I am grateful for that space in his office to open up and tell my story. It is a lesson I remember today as I seek to share my stories in brave spaces long before getting to the point of almost exploding. And it is a lesson I remember today as I seek to live into my calling to work with kids and youth in the context of a solo call to parish ministry.

Chapter Nine

Learning through Unlearning

Sung Hee Chang

> The illiterate of the twenty-first century will not be those who cannot read and write, but those who cannot learn, unlearn, and relearn.

Maybe you've heard this quote before. Do you know whose words they are? If you think you know the answer, you may just wait to see where I am going with it. If not, you might do a Google search. At first glance, most results will refer to the famous futurist Alvin Toffler. You might smile, thinking you got it right. But, like the trivia quiz champion who has recalled correctly, but the knowledge they recalled was incorrect, Toffler is not the author of those exact words. If you are surprised, you may be ready for *unlearning*!

LEARNING TO UNLEARN

In his 1970 book *Future Shock*, envisioning a world where rapid scientific and technological change would drive people crazy, and discussing "education in the future tense," Toffler argued for "instructing students how to learn, unlearn, and relearn" and quoted psychologist Herbert Gerjuoy: "Tomorrow's illiterate will not be the man who can't read; he will be the man who has not learned how to learn."[1] Someone must have read the section on learning in his book and conflated Toffler's with Gerjuoy's words to compose the oft-quoted statement that is set as the epigraph of this chapter. Whether this unnamed person intended it or not, Gerjuoy's and perhaps Toffler's understanding of "learning how to learn" concerns not so much methods, styles, or manners of learning as *the ongoing learning process that consists of learning, unlearning, and relearning.*[2] I contend that Toffler meant that the future learner would become *unlearned* if they did not engage the learning process or, to put it better, the learning *cycle* of learning, unlearning, and relearning.[3]

Half a century later, Toffler's forecast that *the learner will have to learn, unlearn, and relearn in order to become learned* is still apropos. It is true because information or knowledge changes rapidly and thereby becomes obsolete in a very short time. Without unlearning old knowledge, learning new knowledge is difficult if not impossible. Toffler revealed his perspective on learning through unlearning when he wrote, "Students must learn how to discard old ideas, how and when to replace them. They must, in short, learn how to learn."[4] To put it differently, *the learner has to learn how to unlearn in order to learn or relearn or continue to learn*. You can imagine someone who has always worked with a PC starting a new job in an office where everyone is expected to work on a Mac. Of course there are similarities, but a new keyboard and commands require some new learning, which means unlearning the familiar.

Toffler's insight points out an underinvestigated place in education (or learning theories) in general and theological education in particular. Learning theorists should investigate, and we should reflect on as we engage in field education, not only why and how people learn but also *why and how they do not, and even cannot, learn*. What may be getting in the way of growth and learning, impeding our learning? Is it time to risk unlearning?

To be honest with you, many pastors and educators have found it much more difficult to teach the Christian faith to those who have already learned it than to those who have not yet been taught. You can probably picture a know-it-all who resists unlearning in order to learn versus the humble novice who is willing to learn in an unfamiliar field or situation.

Take the example of biblical illiteracy. The problem lies not just in the fact that the vast majority of people do not read the Bible but also in the fact that, when they read it, they read it in order to justify their perspectives rather than to unlearn and learn a new, more faithful perspective. Jesus issues an invitation to all of us to read the Bible with an openness to unlearn when he responds to the lawyer, "What is written in the Law? *What do you read there?*" (Luke 10:26, NRSV, my emphasis). The biblically illiterate of the twenty-first century, in a manner of speaking, are those who have failed to read the Bible (or, to put it better, to be read by the Bible) in such a way that the Bible helps the learner *unlearn* one's own perspective and *learn* God's perspective. In theological field education, transformative learning requires a disposition open to *learning to unlearn*.

THE PROBLEMATIC OF PRIOR KNOWLEDGE

The reality of the learning process is that while there is always something new (desired knowledge) to learn, there is always something old (prior knowledge) to unlearn. And the challenge with the learning-unlearning dialectic is, as the Roman philosopher Seneca the Younger put it, "[our] mind unlearns with difficulty what it has long learned!" What has been learned and has become a habit or second nature in our life dies hard. Unlearning can even be distressing work.

Have you ever visited a country where people drive cars on the "wrong" side of the road? Imagine that you rent and drive a car there. You might think that all you have to do is just *forget* the way you have been driving all your life. But it won't be that easy, for it is "against [your] nature, not against the *laws* of nature," as Mark Twain realized painfully when he tried to learn to ride the penny-farthing (bicycle) for the first time of his life.[5] More than a century later, Destin Sandlin also came to learn the same lesson the hard way while riding the backward brain bicycle that his friend created to tease his brain. He said of his repeated failure in riding this mind-boggling bike, "*My thinking was in a rut* . . . I had the knowledge of how to operate the bike, but I did not have the understanding. Therefore, *knowledge is not understanding*." In order "to prove that [he] could free [his] brain from a cognitive bias," Sandlin spent eight months learning to unlearn how to ride a normal bike. What surprised him (and his viewers as well) at the end of this long and embarrassing experiment was that once he suddenly "could feel some kind of path in [his] brain that was now unlocked" and could ride the backwards bike, he couldn't ride a normal bike anymore! It is interesting to observe that just as he had struggled hard to learn to unlearn how to ride a normal bike, so he had to struggle to unlearn how to ride the backwards bike in order to ride a normal bike again! His advice for his viewers is this: "So be very careful how you interpret things, because *you are looking at the world with a [cognitive] bias*, whether you think you are or not."[6] Learning to unlearn is about changing the way you look at the world.

My point is that unlearning is not so much about forgetting your prior knowledge as it is about changing the mental framework that upholds your prior knowledge.[7] To be more specific, unlearning aims at your conceptual change through a lifelong capacity called *neuroplasticity* in which your brain continuously fine-tunes or rewires itself in response to new experiences (stimuli) for optimal learning. In this learning process, "plasticity" refers to the innate ability of your brain to physically change throughout your lifetime by creating new neural pathways based on sustained focus and repetitive practices. Your brain (your inner gardener) always engages in an unlearning process called *synaptic pruning*, removing the neural connections that are no longer necessary or useful and growing the necessary or useful ones.[8]

Considering our brain's plasticity, learning through unlearning can be said to exemplify what Carol Dweck calls the "growth mindset" (versus the "fixed mindset" that sees your qualities set in stone). To put it differently, to learn through unlearning amounts to learning with an *open mindset* in which we "dare to put what we think we know at risk."[9] In theological field education, in every opportunity to practice the ministerial arts, like preaching and caregiving, you have the opportunity to practice this growth mindset. Reflecting with your supervisor-mentor allows you to interrogate your assumptions, to take the risk of unlearning in order to learn.

PARADIGM SHIFT

The philosophy of science offers another important frame to consider unlearning. As Albert Einstein put it, "We cannot solve our problems with the same thinking we used when we created them." Thomas Kuhn's concept of paradigm shift (or change) addresses this issue squarely. Kuhn noted that science tends to discover what it expects to discover. Discovery comes not when something goes right but *"when something is awry, a novelty that runs counter to what was expected."*[10] Even a scientist has *a tendency to interpret new evidence (a novelty) as confirmation of his or her existing beliefs or theories*! To put it in Einstein's words again, "What a sad era when it is easier to smash an atom than a prejudice."

You probably know the stories of Copernicus and Galileo. Copernicus's mathematical calculations and his observations of the planets' movements could not be aligned exactly. This novelty led to further research from which he posited the theory that placed the sun rather than Earth at the center of the universe. Just before his death in 1543, he published *On the Revolutions of the Celestial Spheres*, a paradigm shift in astronomy. His attention to the new evidence, his unlearning, catalyzed the Copernican revolution, which empowered scientists like Galileo and others to do their paradigm-shifting work. Further anomalies would lead later astronomers to unlearn that our sun is the center of the universe and theorize that there is no center to the universe!

Kuhn's concept of *paradigm change as a result of learning through unlearning* has been applied in other areas of research.[11] Jack Mezirow developed a critical and constructive learning theory mirroring Kuhn's observation on the dynamics of conceptual change in scientific inquiry. Just as Kuhn paid attention to the *anomaly* in scientific research and the emergence of scientific discoveries, so Mezirow identified a disorienting *dilemma*, and the critical assessment of assumptions, ultimately leading to an acute internal and personal *crisis* and exploration of options for new roles with his groundbreaking 1978 study titled *Education for Perspective Transformation: Women Reentry Programs in Community College.*[12]

As a scientific researcher and constructivist, the learning process for Mezirow was not so much the construction of knowledge as it was the transformation of knowledge leading to social action. He defined transformative learning as *"learning that transforms problematic frames of reference to make them more inclusive, discriminating, reflective, open, and emotionally able to change."*[13] It was his conviction, and still is that of those who follow him, that "critical reflection triggers transformative learning."[14] No surprise, then, that our critical reflection in field education may lead to unlearning that yields new frames of reference that foster transformative engagement.[15] Like the scientific paradigm shift, the perspective transformation of the learner occurs *as a result of unlearning initiated by critical reflection.*

Mezirow's transformative learning theory, in essence, is an emancipatory critical theory that uncovers and confronts the hegemonic assumptions of our frames of reference and the power dynamics and relationships among them.[16] He promoted a critically reflective and collaborative dialogic learning and created a learning space where diverse self-directed learners are challenged to examine their practices and underlying assumptions, develop a more inclusive mindset, and understand the experiences and perspectives of others. He believed that in this critical transformative learning process, *the meaning of our experience becomes clarified.*[17]

MOVING TOWARD ENLIGHTENMENT(S)

Another frame of mind from which to wrestle with unlearning is the logic of modern Western Enlightenment reasoning (*sapere aude*, "dare to know"). It assumes that we have total control over our learning process of which the primary goal is to make the world in our image. The learning method is "divide and analyze." And one of its unspoken learning objectives is "learn to divide the world," as John Willinsky puts it. Investigating the close relationship of this self-centered way of learning with modern Western imperialism's "will to know" and its classic policy of "divide and conquer," Willinsky draws our attention to the too often neglected fact that we have inherited uncritically the educational legacy of imperialism. This worldview purports a world still divided subtly and named wrongfully by the Western teaching of history, geography, science, language, literature, and more. As he concludes, this imperialistic educational legacy of *privileging the West and othering the so-called non-West* ("this idea of ourselves as knowing others better than they know themselves") must be unlearned.[18]

Imagine this worldview at work in this encounter:

> A university professor went to visit a famous Zen master. While the master quietly served tea, the professor talked about Zen. The master poured the visitor's cup to the brim, and then kept pouring. The professor watched the

overflowing cup until he could no longer restrain himself. "It's full! No more will go in!" the professor blurted. "This is you," the master replied. "How can I show you Zen unless you first empty your cup?"[19]

What the professor failed to do, as the Zen master implied with his silent action, was to learn to empty his cup before filling it—that is to say, to learn to unlearn in order to learn. No surprise, he was not able to understand the Zen master's action until the latter gave words to it. Preoccupied with what Kosuke Koyama calls "teacher complex,"[20] he did not want to let go of his preconceived ideas about Zen, even though he wanted to better understand Zen!

A Zen master named Bon Soeng points to the same thing from a different angle: "How about admitting the truth that we don't know, and go from there. If we really live that, it changes everything. . . . What we know blocks the truth. Returning to not knowing opens us up."[21]

As we enter new contexts for ministry in theological field education, can you empty your cup to receive the gift that the persons and place have to offer you? Learning through unlearning is a humble and bold attempt to do what Sydney J. Harris called, using another metaphor, "the whole purpose of education," including field education, *to turn mirrors into windows*." Dare to do this turning! *Dare to unlearn!*

QUESTIONS FOR REFLECTION

1. What circumstance were you in where you felt as if you were riding the backward brain bicycle? How did you manage your anxiety and frustration? What did you learn or unlearn from the experience?
2. Imagine that you were the professor who visited a Zen master. Do you think you would be enlightened by the action of the Zen master without his explanation? How would you react to the explanation of the Zen master? Does this story help you understand the meaning of *learning through unlearning*? If so, how?
3. In a famous scene of *Star Wars, Episode V: The Empire Strikes Back*, Luke Skywalker, the novice Jedi who was learning from Jedi Yoda about the ways of the force, had to get his X-wing out of the swamp using the force. About this task, the teacher and the student did not have the same mind. Here is their conversation:

   Luke: Master, moving stones around is one thing. This is totally different.

   Yoda: No. No different. Only different in your mind. *You must unlearn what you have learned.*

Luke: All right, I'll give it a try.

Yoda: No. Try not. Do . . . or do not. There is no try.

(Luke failed, and then Yoda succeeded in lifting up the starfighter.)

Luke: I can't believe it!

Yoda: That's why you failed!

What is the X-wing to be lifted up in your ministry setting? How can you unlearn what you have so far learned about it? Does your faith help you to unlearn?

SUGGESTED READINGS

Thomas S. Kuhn, *The Structure of Scientific Revolutions: 50th Anniversary Edition*, 4th ed. (Chicago: University of Chicago Press, 2012).

Jack Mezirow and Associates, *Learning as Transformation: Critical Perspectives on a Theory in Progress* (San Francisco, CA: Jossey-Bass, 2000).

Aidan Seery and Éamonn Dunne, eds., *The Pedagogics of Unlearning* (Goleta, CA: Punctum Books, 2016).

John Willinsky, *Learning to Divide the World: Education at Empire's End* (Minneapolis: University of Minnesota Press, 1998).

Chapter Ten

Reeducation

William Willimon

"Your greatest challenge, as a young preacher, will be to hide your intellect when you get into the pulpit," said my erstwhile preaching professor. "You are smart. Trouble is, you'll be tempted to show off, swamping them with what you've learned in three years of seminary. A sermon is not a lecture. Get some good ideas. Fine. But when you are in the pulpit, in crafting a sermon, put them on the bottom shelf."

My first year into ministry, I heard a fellow preacher (who served a church larger than mine) brag, "I try to craft my sermons so that they can be easily comprehended by any thoughtful 14-year-old." This, even though his church had few members under 50.

"The task of the preacher is to begin with the biblical text, carefully studying the ancient, Near Eastern context, dig out what the text says, and then leave *all that in your study!*" advised a distinguished preacher who spoke to our annual Clergy Renewal Day. Learn to say what you say in the pulpit so just about anybody can walk away mumbling, "I got it." Put forward the truth of Christ, sure, but put it on the bottom shelf.

When I returned to the parish in 1980 after teaching at Duke Divinity School, the appointing bishop warned me, "You be sure to keep all that professor stuff to yourself. The folks at Northside Church are hardworking blue-collar people who don't want to have all your academic theology dumped on them."

Right. Don't mention the latest book I've read. Hide my intellect. Kill the lecture. Bottom shelf.

Then God sent me Gary to correct my homiletical misunderstanding.

Gary owned a hardware store, and he was a longtime—but not too comfortable—member of Northside United Methodist Church. My first week as pastor, someone warned me about Gary. "He's usually quiet," they said, "but be careful." Then they recalled the Sunday back in 1970 when, in the middle of the sermon (the previous preacher's weekly diatribe against Nixon and the Vietnam war), Gary had stood up from where he was sitting, shook his head, shouted out "Enough already!," and walked right out.

The offending preacher was moved that spring.

So, I always preached with one eye on my notes and the other on Gary. He hadn't walked out on a sermon in more than 10 years. Still, a preacher can never be too safe. Preach Jesus Christ and him crucified, but only after you have tucked him securely on the bottom shelf within easy reach.

You can imagine my fear when one Sunday, having waited until everyone had shaken my hand and left the narthex, Gary approached me, gritting his teeth and muttering, "I just don't see things your way, preacher. I was really bothered by what you said, if I understand correctly what you were trying to say."

I moved into my best mode of nondefensive defensiveness, assuring Gary that my sermon was just one way of looking at things, that we only have 20 minutes to explain things, and that perhaps he had misinterpreted what I said, and even if he had not, I could very well be wrong and er, uh . . . "Don't you back off with me," he snapped. "I just said that your sermon shook me up. I didn't ask you to take it back. Stick by your guns—if you're a real preacher."

Then he said to me, with an almost desperate tone, "Preacher, I run a hardware store. Since you've never had a real job, let me explain it to you. Now, you can learn to run a hardware store in about six months. I've been there *15 years*. That means that all week, nobody talks to me like I know anything. I don't get taken seriously by nobody. Only place I get to think is at church.

"Every Monday, once Zeb and me get the floor swept and all the tools put out front, we sit down and pour ourselves coffee. Zeb will say, 'Well, what did that preacher of yours say this week?'

"So, I pull out the notes I've made on the back of the bulletin and go back through what I remember of the sermon. Zeb listens, asks questions. I try to answer as best I can. Sometimes I just tell Zeb I couldn't make hide nor hair out of what you said.

"Zeb once said, 'I wish our preacher would try to say something worth rememberin'.'

"You see, I'm not like you, don't get to sit around and read books and talk about important things. It's just me and that hardware store. Sunday morning and your sermons are all I've got.

"Please, don't you dare take it back."

Having been tutored by Gary, first thing Monday morning I got into my study and began reading in preparation for my sermon. Gary deserves the highest and best I've got. As I studied, I prayed, "Come on, Lord. Give me something for next Sunday that will stupefy Gary and give him something to chew on all week."

Adapted from *Stories by Willimon* (Nashville, TN: Abingdon, 2020), 23. Used by permission.

Chapter Eleven

Practicing Resurrection

Katie Crowe

Practice resurrection.[1]

I stepped out of the church doors into the waning light of another too-long day and pulled my jacket tight against me to drive back the chill. Looking up at the gray October sky, darkening clouds thick and heavy like boiled wool, I considered my options carefully.

To my left was a 10-minute walk to the local hospital. I could take the main elevator that had carried me to countless pastoral visits with the sick and dying and ride it to the adult behavioral health unit. There I would take off my coat and fold it over my arm, approach the small plastic window that served as a gateway to the admitting nurse on duty, smile, and say politely that I was there to check myself in. My life was out of my control. My thoughts of self-mutilation were out of my control. I was not safe alone.

To my right was a short walk to my car and a 10-minute drive home, where I would be alone for the night, again. My husband traveling for work, again. The growing impulse to cut out the cavernous depression and crippling anxiety for good before me, again. I had a plan.

There was destruction in either direction. To the left, the prospect of social death. People like me didn't check themselves into behavioral health because their lives and thoughts were out of their control. People like me were very much in control and got to where they were because of it. To the right, the prospect of physical death. The thought of which was not nearly as distressing as the awareness of the pain it would cause to the people who loved me who, when I could feel, I had also loved.

Taking a deep breath, face lifted to the sky, I lingered for a moment and turned to the right. A short walk later, I sat in my car, seatbelt buckled, and did something I had never done before and have not done since. I contracted with God. I would go home and go straight to bed if one of two things would happen in the morning. Either God would wake me up with the face and name of the person I was supposed to seek out for help, or God wouldn't. If God did, then I would seek out that person directly. If God didn't, then I would go directly to the hospital and check myself in, and I didn't care which happened. I went home and went to bed.

The next morning, in the fog of that earliest awareness of consciousness before fully waking, there was a face and a name. It was a pastor, formerly affiliated with the church where I served, whom I had interacted with perhaps just three times in as many years, the head of the chaplaincy department of the hospital that wouldn't have the opportunity to admit me. I resolved to seek him out.

That Sunday found him standing outside the church after worship, itself an anomaly. I went up to him and told him how funny it was that he should be there that morning, that he had been on my mind. I needed someone to talk to and wondered if he ever did any counseling. Would he be willing to meet with me? He stood and regarded me for a moment with tenderness in his eyes. Then he smiled and said gently, "Katie, I've been waiting for you for six months."

That pastor and I began a counseling relationship that spanned two and a half years, meeting every two weeks for, at times, hours on end. He refused to allow me to compensate him for his time. He said that it was his gift to the church. The same week as this therapeutic relationship began, the practice of centering prayer, a method of maintaining interior silence to rest in God, found me. The Holy Spirit, through the contemplative silence of centering prayer, started healing me from the inside out, the counseling relationship from the outside in. Their consummation brought forth new life and saved me.

I didn't have a vocabulary for what I was experiencing at the time. Saint John of the Cross might have called it the dark night of the soul, others clinical depression. I only knew that I was increasingly unrecognizable as the person I knew myself to be as a beloved child of God. This compounded my pain with the sense that I was betraying my truest self. None of my education, church life, or professional experiences had framed the interior vulnerabilities that vocational ministry can exploit in the life of the pastor beyond abstractly urging self-care. I would learn the hard way, as so many of my peers do.

Though I was oblivious to it at the time, I had developed a set of assumptions over the course of my young life about myself and ministry, whose cumulative effect contorted my sense of identity, motivation, and perspective on what thriving in service to God and Christ's church was about. These assumptions served as scaffolding for the construction of a maligned value system, and it took nearly losing my life to realize that the center didn't hold.

I had to unlearn a lifetime of lessons and reconstitute my understanding of self and vocation, both personal and professional.

The first lesson that I had to unlearn was that the intellectual exploration of God is synonymous with an experiential encounter with God. I had, through authentic passion for learning, confused the satisfaction that I drew from academic study and serving in God's name with spirituality. Surely the hours spent poring over papers in school, and later writing sermons, preparing Sunday school lessons, counseling parishioners, leading worship, and educating and mobilizing around mission all helped me fall deeper in love with Jesus. But none of them required me to make myself vulnerable to Jesus. Only the introduction of the Christian contemplative tradition would illumine an entirely new pathway to wholeness through spirituality that I had either not previously seen or had been too arrogant to follow.

I have occasionally joked that I possess all the deficits of narcissism without enjoying any of the benefits. As a responsible, driven, achievement-oriented, people-pleasing, workaholic, only-child rule follower, I was quite sure that everything was about me, in that it was all up to me, yet I had never thought particularly highly of myself. This overblown sense of responsibility for the world translated into the lesson that I needed to manage everyone's experience of one another, God, and the church, lest it all fall apart on account of my failure. The overfunctioning that this cultivated in the name of helping others avoid external conflict or confrontation within themselves not only led me to 80-hour work weeks, sleepless fears, panic attacks that dropped me to the floor, and standards of perfection that I could not possibly reach; it also served as an obstacle to the flourishing of the covenant community. I did not know then what I know now, that the Holy Spirit does some of its best work in the lives of individuals and in the building up of the church when the rest of us perceive things to be falling apart or going contrary to plan. As I healed from my impulse to moderate the experience of everyone and the unfolding of everything, I learned that God's grace was sufficient not only existentially but also tactically. The Spirit was a gifted colleague in ministry, whom I could count on to care for Christ's church in ways that were beyond all that I could ever ask for or imagine, let alone achieve. I could rest in this trust.

I had to unlearn the lesson of selflessness, at least in the way that I had come to interpret it. Selflessness as I understand it now is the freedom that comes with forfeiting our fiefdoms and finding our place in God's sweeping love story with creation manifest in Jesus, swimming in the pools of significance, identity, surrender, sacrifice, perspective, and purpose that accompany life with him. My understanding of selflessness then, however, was the act of placing the needs, hopes, priorities, and desires of others always before my own. At its best, this posture helped me recognize my need for humility. At its worst, it led me to humiliation as I shamed my needs, hopes, priorities, and desires into hiding when they emerged, believing that honoring them would be unfaithful. I had to come to terms with the fact that I was part of that creation that God so dearly loved and therefore equally worthy of the acknowledgment and compassion that I sought to extend to others.

The Apostle Paul writes, "I have been crucified in Christ; and it is no longer I who live, but it is Christ who lives in me." Theologically, this is framed as the work of mortification and vivification: putting to death and coming to life. I went into ministry believing that these words were a call to self-renunciation, but I see them now as a call to practice resurrection, to honor the natural drives of the ego for survival, esteem, and control while moderating their cravings by fostering health and balance, lest they become the center of gravity around which life and ministry orbit.

Practicing resurrection now means living daily out of a reordered value system: One that takes Psalm 46:10, with its charge to be still, and know that I am God, seriously. One that believes that my personal flourishing is as much a means of glorifying God and exhibiting the kingdom of heaven on earth as the ministry I seek to embody in pursuit of a thriving church, a just society, and a symbiotic creation. This value system holds as central a cruciform truth that I now understand not just intellectually but also experientially. The truth that the cost of love is letting go—not in a way that leads to the end of life but to fullness of life.

I had to die to my need to be the Creator. But when I did, what came to life was newfound delight in my creatureliness that led me closer to God. As I continue to practice resurrection each day, I find that I encounter Christ more fully within myself and the church. In his deepening presence, I see all the more clearly that vocational ministry is simply life—life in abundance, and life that I want to live.

Chapter Twelve

Meeting My Body through the Grace of Unlearning

Christin Bothe

It seemed random to find myself enrolled in a course about eating disorders during my final semester of divinity school. Sure, perhaps I have experienced levels of "disordered eating," as most of us do, but I have not struggled with body image or eating insecurities in the same way that others I know have. My other three classes for that semester were much more typical for my degree—Christian Ethics, Church History, and a course called Church and Culture. Yet, when I mentioned my fourth class to others, I typically received a curious, raised eyebrow. I still do not know if I could tell you why I took it. Grace, perhaps.

Every Tuesday during these months, I would arrive at a modest room on the third floor of the psychology building to find a small collection of women gathered. A few graduate students, but mostly undergraduate students, were led by our teacher, who was both a practitioner and university professor. The layout of each session was similar. We would take a few moments to get settled, enough time for some small talk with a neighbor or to refresh on the readings we had completed. Each of us had prepared for class the week prior by closely reading three to four studies regarding the given topic, sharing reflections to an online discussion board, and preparing thoughts for the conversation we would have. Additionally, twice during the semester we were responsible for leading the class time. So, quickly after our professor's welcome, she would hand over the lead to someone else.

Topics each week ranged from eating behaviors seen in toddlers, to the role perfectionism plays in eating habits, to the risks that athletes face, to concerns coinciding with gender and sexuality, to ethnic considerations. We dove into the broad-ranging biological, cultural, and relational factors that increase the likelihood of developing an eating disorder. However, we were not gathering to find a cure, or eliminate it, or even discover the perfect intervention. We were simply there to learn more about what this complex illness was, why it might be so prevalent, and why some treatments have, or have not, been successful. Nestled within a bustling research university, our small class of women sat together and sought to understand forces and circumstances that were unavoidably personal to each of us. This disorder pointed our attention to a shared wound that beckoned our whole selves—not just our minds but our bodies, emotions, and past experiences as well.

I would guess that each of us knew what we wanted to believe—that our bodies were intrinsically good, that we didn't need to achieve a certain size or appearance or feeling to be content with who we were. Yet, each of us was familiar with the sentiment of knowing our bodies as not "enough." Our teacher, humbly, did her best to create a course that could handle all these tensions. We learned, but we did so with a slowness that allowed the learning to sink deep within us. We approached each topic with care and patience. It modeled for me what tending to my body might feel like—a patience in noticing, wondering about, accepting, and sharing.

With each week, I found myself invited to reflect on various personal circumstances and experiences. As we learned about the fragile relationship a mother shares with her daughter, I thought about the ways the absence of my biological mother in my adolescent years may have both positively and negatively affected the ways I related to my body. When we took time to learn about specific sports that encourage thinness, I thought back to the years I spent running cross country and the teammate I had been close to who developed anorexia nervosa. When we talked about perfectionism, I remembered a friend from college who used obsessive eating habits to feel in control amid the chaos of being far from home. Similarly, when the biological factors were presented, I discovered language to express why certain warning signs were not always present in those I knew, as some are more predisposed to this illness. Slowly unpacking each topic created this unforeseen space to understand my past in light of the numbers and statistics that sat within the research we examined.

These connections granted me new insights, but more than that, I was finding grace and patience to extend to myself. I did not need a diagnosis to admit that I, too, had a lot to learn about treating my body with love. Pulling up these moments helped me to acknowledge that I never had been taught how to do that. Few of us in that room had. We shared a vulnerability to the questions we confronted, as none of us had been immune from the distortions that are hidden at the core of eating disorders. Ironically enough, the most profound steps forward we discovered came from the voices and experiences of those who seemed to be the most battered from this illness. Their stories of healing held insight we needed for our studies and our own lives.

It sounds taboo to stand in front of a mirror and "examine" your body—slowly moving your attention to each curve and feature, just noticing how you feel. Yet, this practice is one of many that I was drawn to and gifted by. In treatment, this exercise is used for women who may have developed an attentional bias contributing to their illness. Perhaps they were hyperfocused on their thighs or stomach and stopped being able to see these parts in perspective to the rest of their body. This practice allows attention to be retrained to see the body in its entirety, and it models how to hold fear and doubt, but also courage and sensitivity, in relating to one's body.

When we had first encountered this as a proposed intervention, I was surprised by how relieved I felt. I grew up watching siblings and friends take hours to stare at themselves in mirrors, seeming unsatisfied, as they put on makeup or tried on different outfits. So often, I saw this behavior as vain and selfish. In wanting to relate to my body in a different way, I took to the other extreme—avoiding any concern about my body. In effect, I often felt distant from myself. I resisted looking at my reflection with any sense of care and punished myself when I worried about how I looked or what I was wearing. Learning from this practice helped me realize that there was a middle ground between these two extremes. Mirrors had become something I associated with vanity instead of seeing them as a tool to know myself in a truthful way, or even as a means to gratitude through careful observance. In rejecting this previous understanding, I was able to appreciate that being attentive to my body is a sacred activity—not one I should punish myself, or others, for. Naming this invited me to embrace a kinder way of relating to others and to recognizing myself.

Additionally, I learned about the media literacy classes that are often part of treatment and recovery. These courses aim to help cultivate an awareness of the manipulation that occurs in advertisements and in other forms of media. Students are taught to identify a marketing strategy at work while also pausing to check in with themselves. How did they feel being exposed to that image, even though they know it was manipulative? Was there any shame or embarrassment felt? Validating these emotions becomes a way to proactively navigate the hidden stress that can emerge in negative actions later.

As I read studies about this treatment model, I became aware of the ways I often suppress emotions that come from such everyday experiences. I see women who are tanner, skinnier, curvier, and prettier than myself on posters in stores or in advertising. In efforts to not be emotionally impacted, I have chosen to focus my attention on how smart I am, or how athletic I am, so I do not have to deal with insecurities I have about my body. Acknowledging this uncovered a dangerous dichotomy I have created in believing I am above those who care more about being attractive than I do. While culture may attempt to manipulate beauty to make money, I was perpetuating the lies that were already being wrapped around these women. Beauty is a part of our createdness that can and should be celebrated. I tried to understand my dignity as separate from beauty or appearance. In doing so, I fragmented my dignity instead of embracing its many parts. Media literacy has provided me with language to understand my distance from this truth and has revealed a path for me to learn how to engage with such everyday images in a way that honors those in them and myself.

One of the surveys we encountered in our seminar confirmed that women tend to understand their physical appearance to be where their bodies find value. Men, on the other hand, typically find it in the functionality their bodies exhibit. Having engaged with my resistance to nurturing my physical appearance, I found that my fear has kept me entangled in this belief. In trying to disregard it, I had let it keep its control. Both appearance and functionality are vital aspects in understanding the reality each of our bodies hold. Yet, our value is not based on them—it is, indeed, intrinsic. In my efforts to escape these characteristics, I had failed to find what lay beneath. It will be in my journey to accept them that I will have the courage to recognize something surpassing and richer.

Ultimately, I found myself with tools and practices to believe that I was made "good." I had grown up hearing that in church and reading it in the Bible. I believed it was true, but the assurance was purely a mental activity. It was finally during this course that I found evidence for the ways culture has distorted my ability to experience, or feel, this truth. The facts, research, and dialogue combined with the slowness, vulnerability, and care had manifested in learning that reached sensitively into the knowledge and experiences I had walked into the classroom with. Our professor's method of teaching engaged with what each of us had already, consciously or unconsciously, learned.

I watched this course transform the ways I saw myself, and I witnessed it transform the ways I participated in my other classes. I found myself in Christian Ethics more convinced that the weak, or "the diagnosed," might have something to teach us about how to live the good life. In Church History I reflected more deeply on the ways the church was a wounded, broken body within its deep division—yet, I had a newfound hope that healing was possible. In my course Church and Culture, I found that conversations on the church's relationship with media interested me, and alarmed me, in completely new ways.

As the semester closed, I found myself with this small group of women one last time to reflect and to receive some closing remarks from our professor. Her role had been so limited, yet she had gifted us with a space each of us desperately needed. Together, we watched both academic and personal collide as our minds and bodies found unity in our work. We took a self-reflective look at the distortions that have made eating disorders so prevalent and personal to most women. In the process, I found that sometimes the people we think we know better than are the very ones who can point us toward learning what we need to unlearn.

Chapter Thirteen

Learning through Seeing and Naming

Intersectionality and Theological Field Education

Mark Chung Hearn

One of the high points of theological education, as strenuous and rigorous as it may be, is your theological field education, which some of your institutions might refer to as supervised ministry, field education, internships, contextual education, or some other similar description. As others lay out elsewhere in this book, theological field education utilizes an action-reflection-action model and provides learners an opportunity to engage praxis—critically reflective practice—so that you will reengage ministry with affirmation about who you are and what you do. You will also receive constructive feedback that helps you act, think, and behave differently. Many students often end their theological field education experience with a better-informed ministerial, vocational, and religious sensibility than before they started. This includes increased knowledge in a field, opportunities for personal formation, the accumulation of practical skills, the integration of theory with practice, and deep meaning making. There is not enough space to address all of these, but I will comment briefly on meaning making, particularly as it illuminates the theory of intersectionality.

Educational theorists posit that meaning making is a central concern of adult education.[1] That is, adult learners are particularly drawn to how they make sense of their world—its products, structures, and values—and how they consider new knowledge and experiences that they encounter. Even if, during your theological education, you have not found yourself mumbling under your breath, "What is significant about this experience or theory in light of what I already know and am committed to?" it is likely that you already engage this question with your (subconscious) intellect, spirit, soul, and body. A hospital chaplaincy student who for the first time accompanied a family through the unexpected death of their father and husband is now negotiating her own theological commitments around death and dying as well as her own family roles and responsibilities. These structures are made up of embedded, and usually unconscious, assumptions that offer a congruence to her sense of self, identity, vocation, and the world around her. These structures and assumptions, called meaning frames, are the lens through which new experiences and knowledge are filtered. And when the structures are met with noticeable force or difference (e.g., seeing a patient die before you; witnessing firsthand the raw anger of an anti- or pro-*xyz* group rally), your meaning frames can either shut down, thereby reestablishing your current frame, or open with curiosity to this unknown reality with the prospects of adjusting or creating a new frame.

This opportunity for adjustment often occurs when our experiences or learning especially demand the presence of our whole selves. Though educators do not wish discomfort or the lack of safety for learners, trauma, crisis, and watershed moments are ripe for growth and expanding our meaning frames. Good educators do not shy away from these moments to reflect on and engage with what might be going on for the learner. But what about theological field education that seems more mundane, innocuous, and straightforward? What opportunities exist for equally significant meaning making and learning to occur when trauma and crises are the outlier and not the norm?

INTERSECTIONALITY

I learned about intersectionality theory during my graduate studies and have since incorporated it into my educational tool kit. Though many definitions exist, most agree that intersectionality is a way to analyze and understand the "complexity in the world, in people, and in human experiences."[2] Our intricate world cannot be understood through any one lens. A person working with incarcerated youth, for instance, must study immigration, family systems, and economic patterns to have a more complete understanding of this social subgroup.

Similarly, intersectionality is a powerful instrument for theological field education because it highlights varied meaning-making possibilities and gives texture to the many nuances that exist in any given learning space. The theory offers learners rich possibilities for thinking about why certain realities exist as they do and how people interpret those same things differently. Each case study, no matter how mundane it might seem, holds the capacity for deep critical reflection not only because of the varied learning styles among a group of learners but also because of the array of meaning-making frames that derive from the vast number of experiences and intersecting identities that exist among that very group. The peers in your field education cohort do not come from the same backgrounds, experiences, and meaning frames as you. Therefore, the more routine experiences we have as learners are not experienced or interpreted in the same way by all. Coming to class, reading shared texts, listening to lectures, and discussing critical incidents does not make the same meaning for every learner given that our assumptions, frames, and experiences differ from one another. Moreover, the way race, gender, class, and other social identifiers are socially constructed within specific contexts, such as regions within the United States, contribute to different lived experience and, consequently, different meaning making.

While there is some controversy around the introduction of intersectionality into the academic mainstream, the concept has been particularly helpful in analyzing concrete realities of different people.[3] In her analyses of employment, violence, and abuse, Kimberlé Crenshaw, a law professor and scholar, kept coming up against the very real differences black women and other women of color faced compared to white women or men. She concluded that a sole analysis of race (antiracism) or gender (feminism) was not enough to shed light on the data she collected because these alone failed to tell the whole story and consider the nuances helpful to understanding more fully people's lived realities. The analysis of a black or Southeast Asian woman's experience with employment could not be misappropriated with the analysis of a white woman's experience or that of a male. The mutual and collective consideration of these social identifiers provides an altogether different analysis.

With intersectionality, we now have the capacity to see and consider multiple realities simultaneously.[4] With intersectionality, we are afforded the ability to perceive how structures keep certain people from living abundantly while others have easier access to it. With intersectionality, an individual is not a woman nor Asian alone. She is female, Korean, heterosexual, cisgender, immigrant, and a divorced, middle-aged parent—all at the same time—and cannot be read or understood through a reductionist lens that views her *only* as a woman.[5] Intersectionality cautions theological field education to resist simplifying any meaning-making analysis of a student's concrete experience. Rather, deeper critical exploration in theological reflection should offer you an opportunity to reflect on how you exist and act in a given situation given your intersecting identities, as well as the opportunity for your peers to reflect on how this situation might differ given their intersecting identities. This type of exploration and analysis provides a more comprehensive way to view the meaning-making process and what may go on for people in class reflection.[6]

MY INTERSECTIONAL IDENTITIES AND TEACHING

Let me share a concrete example of how this theory has played out for me as a professor and theological educator. At the end of my first year of full-time teaching, I was in a week-long intensive course with quite a diversity of religious commitment and tradition among our group. We were charismatic Pentecostal, progressive and conservative mainline, Catholic, Evangelical, Unitarian Universalist, and spiritual but not religious. During the break of one of our sessions, a student approached me and asked if we could pray for one of our fellow class members regarding the loss that morning of a family member. I agreed but admittedly with internal trepidation. In this progressive institutional context, how was I to lead this time of prayer? Do I use God-specific language that is comfortable for me and, at the same time, could potentially alienate those in the room who do not hold to a theistic spirituality or faith? Do I close the prayer "in Jesus's name," knowing that there are students who do not see Jesus in the same manner as I do?

Returning once again to meaning making, I find that good learning comes not only in the form of rich content but also in the shape of conscious and aware meta-processing. After the break, I brought up the student's request to the class, and before we prayed, I offered my own hesitation and posed a question: "How many of you are afraid to pray publicly here at the School of Theology and Ministry?" Hands shot up all over the room. "I'm afraid of offending others" and "I fear saying the wrong thing theologically" were two shared answers that received the most agreement and head-nodding approval. We discussed our fears and eventually filled up a whole whiteboard wall of names, needs, and issues for which we would join in prayer together as a community.[7] We prayed; at times it was awkward. But in the end, there was something very sacred about the class coming together in both fear and caution to offer prayer in our own genuine theological voice and faith language.

This reflection could stand alone as an example of navigating through the challenges of learning amid religious pluralism, but there is more with regard to intersectionality. An educator who may not see all the nuances of social and power dynamics at play could simply ask why all the fuss? *After all, are you not the educator and the one in charge? Students are to follow your lead.* While a pedagogical approach exemplifying this philosophy might questionably work, for the sake of our discussion, I draw attention to my own positionality and intersectionality.[8] As a first-year educator who identifies, among other identities, as a progressive Evangelical, United Methodist, cisgender, heterosexual, and Korean American male, I came to a crossroads that day in class. Would I pray as I comfortably do in my Evangelical and Korean American spiritual heritage, which is depicted with words such as "extemporaneous," "Christocentric," "warm," "charismatic," "feel it in your gut," and "soulful"?

Three concerns played in the background for me especially with regard to context. First, how would I present as an Evangelical in a progressive theological institution? I had done my work that first year to build bridges and to not come off as the religious fundamentalist for whom many often mistakenly co-opt Evangelicals.[9] One might say I earned a lot of "street cred" that first year among students and colleagues for my demonstration of critical thoughtfulness, curiosity, and openness that many assume Evangelicals lack.

A second concern I held was that in the larger religious context of the city of Seattle, I was slow to publicly claim my Evangelical heritage as one of my intersecting identities. Shortly after I began my position, a prominent Evangelical pastor in the area went through a notable and public split with the church he helped to plant. For some, the Evangelical pastor was a megachurch icon, while for others he was the epitome of a deadly brand of Christianity. Would I "out" myself and potentially have others misinterpret who I am in light of a particular expression of one identity—Evangelical—during my first year of teaching here?[10]

My third concern gets right to the core of intersectionality theory. Could I afford to claim another minoritized identity in this specific institutional context and be mixed in with this Evangelical pastor though his and my faith commitments are different? Contrary to what some might think, I am not only an educator with privilege who teaches at our school. Though I do hold positional power and the authority of an educator, I am a younger-looking (though I am close to 50), Asian, male, nontenure-track, junior-titled faculty member, which, considered together, can often feel vulnerable.[11] It is far different to analyze and interpret a situation that moves from seeing a person as a (male) faculty member to a faculty member with all these intersecting identities in a historically white and progressive educational institution. It would be remiss to simply lump me in with another colleague who is a white, male, tenured, older full professor entrenched in progressive faith commitments by conjoining us under the label "faculty." Correspondingly, you are not only a student who reflects on your ministerial identity and experiences. You are this and much more. You are a Latina immigrant whose primary language is not English, who has traversed academic terrain to reflect on the cases you and your peers bring. These intersecting identities give clues not only to the makeup of learners we have in a class (i.e., diversity) but, more pointedly, to the complexity of meaning making that exists among learners. We see, experience, and interpret much differently given all of who we are. Joyce del Rosario's teaching awareness of intersecting identities allows her to name not only her own identities and positionality but also that of her students such that they affirm her ability to fully see them as multifaceted people. Her students trust her ability and desire to see them in their fullness.

Similarly, mindful of all your intersecting identities, I imagine that your educational journey and experience throughout seminary takes on meanings different from those of any of your learning colleagues. The way you experience your supervised ministry is different than it would be for another peer were they to intern at the same site and position. Therefore, it is important in a learning setting for you to identify your, and your colleagues', intersectional identities. Each person makes meaning differently, and this provides learners with a far greater panoply of analysis, motivation, and response.

Paulina Alvarado, a chaplain, recalls an episode of a room visit she had with an out-of-control male patient. As a caregiver in profession and vocation, she considers how her own intersecting identities of Catholic, Latina, chaplain novice, and having previous exposure to domestic violence, influences her own (in)ability to respond with care. As a chaplain, she is called to care, but what are the challenges to providing care given her intersecting identities? She also wonders whether the patient would have responded differently to her if the chaplain was somebody else with different social identifiers. These questions and reflections would not be as nuanced if a class analysis of this case study only considered a chaplain identity. Delimiting the interpretation to this one identity would severely hamper a full reflection of the dynamics that exist for the learner in a case study such as this.

CHALLENGES TO THE THEORY

Understandably, a person might critique this approach as divisive because it seems to diverge from identifying common ground among a community of learners. *Your experience and meaning making is so far different from mine that I find no resonance with it and, thus, feel further away from you, not closer. So why use this theory if I feel more distant?* I take this concern seriously as one might conclude that there is the potential for tribalism and siloed learning. I respond with a couple of reflections.

First, Emmanuel Lartey brings to our attention a "trinitarian formulation of personhood," a concept derived from the 1948 work of Clyde Kluckholn and Henry Murray. This is Lartey's formulation:

> I am like all others.
> I am like some others.
> I am like no others.[12]

There is something about the human experience and condition that binds humanity together with one another. We feel; we hurt; we smile. Yet, culturally, there is something we might experience and understand with only a group of others. The experience is not shared with all humanity, though it remains a full human experience. Finally, there are only certain experiences and thoughts that are uniquely one's own due to one's physical and psychosocial characteristics.[13] To this last point, I add that the construction of one's social location and positionality, combined with their individual characteristics, contribute to the unique existence and lens no other individual can quite match. Community learners hold a tension between living as fellow human kin and discovering how the human experience is also distinct.

In her case memoir, Shaina Williams helps us see how her experiences of black communities have been both alienating and healing as a young black woman. Her internship experience working with other black women has become a healing balm and an inspiration to better understand herself and the women with whom she works. She continues to see others and herself more completely because of the common *and* unique experiences of the other women at the internship. Her story of healing would be incomplete if we only saw her internship as an experience with other women as a member of humanity rather than as a black woman who resonates with, and yet differs from, other black women. By drawing attention to the specifics of her intersecting identities, we are not judging her nor advocating for a racist stance. Rather, we do the opposite. We advocate for anti-oppression through capturing her experiences and opening ourselves up to a more comprehensive understanding of ministerial and leadership formation. Bringing attention to these nuances draws us nearer to the fullness of kin-dom seeing.

Emile Townes raises a second and similar thought for theological (field) education: a crucial turn toward particularity.[14] When you articulate your particularity and are taken seriously in it, there is room for further deepening of understanding. During a case study presentation of one of my own experiences as a young pastor just out of seminary, I shared with the class how a parent of a dying toddler requested that I pray for their child to be healed. While most of the progressive mainline students held a pastoral theology of presence (i.e., one's ministerial presence, rooted in incarnational theology, is enough), a black, conservative, Pentecostal, Methodist pastor pushed back on the overwhelming theology of the group and offered a counter reflection that we have no idea of God's workings. She, in her particular and intersecting identities, was able to help the group consider a different theological commitment than what most held. Consequently, we had a far richer discussion that touched on several different ministerial responses thanks to this student living into her theological and cultural beliefs around prayer and healing. Particularity does not have to result in a power play, as if one's unique experience and lens is all that matters. Rather, the power of particularity (and intersectionality) demands and affords the opposite. We can now be a community in ways that are not as possible if the approach to learning only generalizes and universalizes the human experience. When we open discussions in theological field education to the particular, we nurture curiosity and openness to the comprehensive movement of the Spirit of God at work in, and throughout, humanity.

CONCLUDING REMARKS

I name the chapter "Learning through Seeing and Naming" because there is an element of prophetic truth telling intersectionality requires and brings. There is something to be said about the capacity to see and name rightly something for what it is and not for what we think it ought to be. There are many instances of Jesus's ability to see people for who they were (the woman with the alabaster jar, Zacchaeus, the Canaanite woman, the widow with the two coins) when others, who followed or kept a watchful eye on Jesus, were unwilling to do the same. One of my favorite healing narratives comes in the Gospel of Mark, where Jesus heals a blind man at Bethsaida (Mark 8:22–26). Jesus spits on a blind man's eyes, and a curious exchange ensues. "Can you see anything?" Jesus asks, to which the man replies, "I can see people, but they look like trees, walking" (Mark 8:23–24).[15] Jesus lays his hands on the man's eyes a second time, and the narrative states that he now saw things clearly.

Grasping this theory of intersectionality offers you and I an opportunity to see more clearly the truth of people's lives, including our own. As Jesus's healing does not occur on the first go-around, learning this theory and its impact requires time. It takes commitment to identify and articulate our own social identities and then to see how the intersection of these identities plays out in any given context and situation. It also calls for as much attention to the intersectional identities of others and to ask, in honoring dialogue, how one interprets and responds to a situation in their self-identification.

So, I encourage you to do your own work in uncovering and naming your intersectional identities. After you have done this, ask how these identities, which are always present and mutually reinforcing, influence your experience and read of a situation or case study. Finally, raise the question in your reflection groups of how each person's intersectional identities might contribute to the group's reflection. When we commit to this theory and work, it transforms our learning and meaning making in theological field education.

QUESTIONS FOR REFLECTION

1. How do you socially identify? What situations or contexts highlight one or more social identifiers over the others? For instance, my gender, parental status, and academic education are much more prominent in a Korean American context than is my race or ethnicity, which are more prominent at work and in society.
2. Think of another person you know well, and take a quick inventory of their intersecting identities (race, gender, class, religion, body type, etc.). Now think of a recent case study. How might your experience of

this case study compare or contrast with this other person's were they to be in the same situation as you? Make this comparison with two or more identifiers. How might this situation compare with someone who holds vastly different intersectional identities than yours?
3. In question 2 above, consider your reflection again, but only through one lens (e.g., race). How does using only one identity, rather than intersecting identities, affect your analysis?

SUGGESTED READINGS

Patricia Hill Collins and Sirma Bilge, *Intersectionality* (Cambridge: Polity, 2016).

Patricia R. Grzanka, *Intersectionality: A Foundations and Frontiers Reader* (Boulder, CO: Westview, 2014).

Ange-Marie Hancock, *Intersectionality: An Intellectual History* (New York: Oxford University Press, 2016).

Chapter Fourteen

Thank You for Seeing Me

Joyce del Rosario

When I started my first semester as a professor, I found myself worrying. I spent the last four years asking one narrow research question in my doctoral studies, and suddenly I was tasked to help MDiv students navigate their vocational calls in the Field Education class. I was trained to research, but was I trained to teach a subject outside of my field? I quickly learned that I would need to rely on not just my theoretical training but also my lived praxis. Additionally, I would need to use what I have learned in my praxis through the lens of my social location. I am particularly conscious of my social location because in theological education I tend to be an outlier as a cisgender, heterosexual, single, Filipina American scholar who describes her faith tradition as a progressive charismatic Evangelical United Methodist. How much would I be able to identify with my students? It turns out, quite a bit.

My class is an array of social identities. They identify as Latinx, African American, white, and Pacific Islander. They are recovering addicts, formerly incarcerated, formerly fundamentalist, and formerly agnostic. They are urban, suburban, and rural. They are LGBTQ, cisgender, heterosexual, divorced, married, never married. Each person has their own unique and rich story of becoming, and we have committed in this year-long class to journey together in discovery of what their next life chapters will look like.

Imposter syndrome hit me hard the first few classes. What if they realize I don't know a lot of things? What if they realize my degree didn't prepare me for this class? I needed to pivot and recalibrate my understanding of what made me an expert in field education, the guild in which few of us are specifically trained.

I have learned that as a woman of color, I must survive academia by digging deeper into myself. As a result, I teach from an *embodied epistemol-*

ogy. I identify embodied epistemology as a source of knowing and teaching from our intersectional selves. My brown skin, gender, height, faith tradition, vocational experience, cultural awareness, and family upbringing are all a part of the location from whence I teach. This type of epistemology is not often considered in academia that has traditionally favored philosophical and theoretical rationality over emotions and experience. For people of color, particularly women of color, we cannot escape our objectified bodies, so we see the world through all of who we are. In womanist terms, it includes our race, class, gender, and sexuality. In all my academic training, I often felt less capable than my white male counterparts. In doctoral seminars, my white male colleagues often spoke with intellect and confidence, rendering my intuitive embodied epistemology inferior to their mastery of other theologians in mainly white male canons. So, I learned their canons, I learned their vocabulary, and I learned their methodologies. But when I am at my pedagogical best, I teach from all of who I am, from my embodied epistemology.

In one class we held a theological panel. We shared who we are, how we arrived at our theologies, and how our theologies inform our praxis. It was on this panel where I began to share more freely how I have come to integrate my being Filipinx and a woman in an academic system built for someone else. I have not accomplished anything alone, and I do not stand on the teaching platform alone. I approach both my praxis and theology along with my ancestors and with my extended family. I teach from all the relationships past and present that have informed who I am today.

For example, I am a Filipina shaped by the ideas of *pakikisama* (fellowship) and *kapwa* (belonging). This understanding of shared identity is the class environment I seek to create. That is not to say that we are all the same but that we are all gathered with the understanding that we have each other's best in mind. When we bring our authentic selves to the classroom and can share and appreciate in each other's authentic expressions, the whole class benefits from communal learning. This is distinct from an individualist, prove-what-I-know approach to pedagogy.

It's important that we recognize our intersectionality as educators because that embodied epistemology will resonate with the diversity of students pursuing theological education today. The more we understand ourselves and not just our subject matters, the more we can teach from the fullness of our beings.

I know this approach to teaching is important because of a moment we experienced in our class about two-thirds into the semester. I had the students take turns doing an opening centering activity each class. One of the students led us through an affirmation ritual. We were instructed to pick one of the cards that were spread face down on the table in front of us. Once we picked the card, we were to pass it around without having looked at it. The other students could look at the card, each marked with an image and word, and then consider what of the image sparked words of encouragement about the person in the hot seat. Then they would share their encouraging thoughts with the person in the hot seat. At the end, the person in the hot seat could look at the card they picked and consider how their classmates connected them to what they saw on the card.

Each student took a turn in the hot seat. When it was my turn, I carefully chose a card that seemed to be buried at the bottom of a few other cards. I saw the corner of it under a stack and knew I wanted to bring that one up to the surface. Without looking at it, I handed the card to Chuy.[1] Chuy looked at the card and smiled. He seemed to connect with whatever was on the card. Then he carefully passed it to the next student. Each student received the card, spent a little time thinking about what they would say, and then passed it along until it came back around to me.

At this point they were able to share words of encouragement based on the card that everyone but me had looked at. Chuy mentioned how he watched me pick my card. I know he noticed how I looked for the card buried under the others. In a previous conversation with Chuy, I told him, "I'm always looking for those who are trying to fly under the radar."

For many years, I was the one who flew under the radar. Even if I wanted to be noticed, I would still go unnoticed. But most of the time, I was comfortable not being noticed because at least it meant that I didn't have to stick out or explain myself to people who didn't understand my culture, my gender, or my size (I'm just under five feet tall). As I've gotten older and more comfortable in my skin, I look for others who try to fly under the radar, like Chuy. Chuy tries to lay low, but his personality is so whimsical it's difficult to miss him. Covered in tattoos, Chuy is a Chicano student who has seen his unfair share of difficulties in life. He is a single parent who is working to raise his child differently than he was raised. He watched me carefully pick the card at the bottom of the stack because he knew that's part of my pedagogy, to bring to light those who go unnoticed.

During my office hours, Chuy and I chat about his theological and vocational formation, but I mostly spend time hearing him share his story. We spend time bringing to light things about his intersectional epistemology that often get overlooked in academic discourse. His experiences in gangs and incarceration are all part of how he sees things, how he knows things, and how he theologizes, which therefore informs his ministry praxis. This takes time to uncover. This takes patience to listen. This takes intention to meet with him to help him connect his narrative to the theoretical frameworks of the academy. This takes choosing the card at the bottom of the stack.

He smiled again as he thought about what he would say to me. "This is the perfect card. You are about to go to your first academic conference as a professor. I'm so excited for you! This is a new thing for you." He voiced his excitement to see a brown woman scholar enter new spaces where very few

Filipinx women exist. We have a mutual respect for each other's work and the spaces we inhabit because we know there are so few people like us in our fields. We both believe that as we diversify the spaces we are called into, we create new spaces where others will find acceptance as well. We celebrate each other's milestones. This is the joy of seeing one another in our dynamic selves. This is the joy of *pakikisama* and *kapwa*. A win for one of us is a win for all of us.

The other students passed the card around and shared their affirming thoughts. When it landed on Kendra, she smiled a knowing smile like Chuy. Kendra began to share beautiful words of affirmation. She recalled our first conversation, where we shared our love of *lumpia* (Filipino eggroll), Filipino culture, growing up in the 1980s, and other shared commonalities. She recalled how much we connected in that first meeting. We had so much in common even though we're quite different. Kendra is a married, lesbian, African American woman with children. She brought up the conversation because it highlighted how much we could connect as women of color. She ended with this statement: "Your intersectionality helps you see my intersectionality. Thank you for seeing me." She asked for a hug. Then Chuy got up and asked for a hug and also said, "Thank you for seeing me." At this point there were hugs all around the classroom as we experienced a deep connection with one another.

When all was said and done, I turned the card over to see what they had been basing their words on. On the card was a picture of a street running vertically and one horizontally. The word "crossroad" was placed in the middle. I realized that Chuy and Kendra reinterpreted the word "crossroad" as "intersection." My connection to them as a professor was not a crossroad where a decision had to be made about which way to turn; it was an intersection where all roads converge and where we meet with one another. They did not see us at a crossroads where we would soon depart; they saw us meeting at the intersections within our embodied epistemologies and with one another. They thanked me for seeing them in their intersections and celebrated the intersections from which I taught.

"Thank you for seeing me" might be the highest praise I can hope for as a professor. It means that I was able to give of myself authentically and wholly while they were able to receive it in their authentic, whole selves. When I did the theological panel, I tried my best to show them my multidimensional self. I told them about all the facets of my theology. Giving them my authentic self meant that they didn't need to code switch when they talked to me; they could be themselves.

While our school is progressive and diverse in its student body, I realized that Chuy and Kendra were telling me that they haven't felt fully seen in the larger context of our institution. When educators teach from only a gender lens or social class lens, or any other singular lens, we miss out on the students who are robust and transforming beings. Teaching with an intersectional epistemology allows educators like me to see students in their whole beings, name those intersections as gifts that inform their praxis, and join them on their journeys with all of who I am as well.

QUESTIONS FOR REFLECTION

1. Academic rigor is often equated with only intellectual astuteness. Joyce del Rosario resists this idea and offers that embodied teaching, which claims all of one's identities and epistemologies (i.e., how one knows what they know), is equally and perhaps more difficult to do well in teaching. How do you understand rigor in seminary? In (your) theological field education?
2. In the best sense of community sharing, what would you say to your seminary or theological field education program to help them more clearly see students in their intersecting and embodied identities?
3. What, and how, would you share with your theological field education professor about the importance of your intersecting identities?

Chapter Fifteen

More Than Meets the Eye

Paulina Alvarado

Here I am in the emergency room by myself on a cold morning that turned out to be more eventful than I could have imagined. My well-planned day is suddenly disrupted by this busy environment in which I am immersed; a frightening screaming and an escalating yelling push me to what seems the lonely middle of chaos, the disorienting eye of the storm. I feel confused, alone, and as if my already small body was increasingly shrinking. I am a chaplain witnessing this adult male patient unleash his shock, pain, and frustration. My role calls me to be present to those who suffer, yet this scene challenges me to be present even to my own self. A force within is brought to the fore, and it pulls me to a paralyzing edge beyond this immediate situation. I manage to carry on and minister to him.

While I debrief this incident later, many questions come to the surface. Each one unsettles me, as they do not seem to name what I am trying to process: Did I have an emotional reaction because I am a woman facing an intensely out-of-control male? Is it because I am somewhat new to being a chaplain? Is it because I have an accent and an appearance that puts me at a disadvantage from the patient and staff in the room? Or would it be the patient's rejection of religion while I am a Catholic chaplain? Was this a reminder of similar experiences I had as a woman in a South American macho society? Or is it due to my previous exposure to domestic violence?

Although I could confidently answer "yes" to most of these questions, each, taken individually, only points to an isolated analysis of the situation. Stating that I am a Latina does not convey even one of the many interacting parts of my identity. That sole aspect of myself perhaps might call to mind the general oppression that many Latinos have undergone, but it would not reflect, for instance, the particular history of oppression that I withstood in my country of origin, Chile. Together with my gender and age, and therefore my generation, one could more specifically point to a few elements that informed my emotions in the emergency room. Echoes of patriarchy and dictatorship become more intimidating to one who was the youngest child, and a girl, in a dysfunctional household. Combining this with the many other elements that form my worldview, one could perhaps begin to understand why single-lens answers would not significantly capture my whole being in that scenario.

I could not help but wonder, "What if, in this same scenario, the chaplain were a Caucasian woman? How would she have been impacted?" As much as I would like to know the answers, her gender and race would tell us only a little more than gender or race alone. These two, though important, might prevent us from knowing more completely the person, their history, and how this intersects with their learning and responses in a specific situation. There is more to one's existence than meets the eye, and there is more to anyone's experience than one or two visible aspects or angles alone. There is an intersection of different elements, dimensions, in a specific context. We can propose that those dynamics would have been very different if the same episode took place in a hospital in Chile or if this would have happened prior to my theological education and spiritual formation. No single characteristic could express wholly who I am as a person (e.g., my ethnicity alone cannot be the answer to my emotions). Is a person not more than a racial being? Than a gendered being? Than one's past or current context alone? Am I not more than my religion or my professional trajectory in that visit to this person?

It may be clearer now why those initial questions and conjectures, however accurate, left me feeling unacknowledged and overwhelmed: different identities of who I am were examined in isolation as if arbitrarily taken apart to make them answer to this particular scenario. This approach of single-lens analysis discounts the whole unique person I am in moments such as this. Indeed, it is precisely because of my unique past involving oppression, violence, and disregard in Chile and in my family of origin that a perceived indifference for my total self becomes overwhelming and confusing.

Certainly, from just a medical care standpoint, we can value the regard for the whole person and their particular context. As a patient, we may know that each aspect of our lives will be accounted for. One cannot receive proper care unless all important factors, their interrelatedness, the conditions of the medical issue, and the occurrences at the time of the visit are contemplated together. No one consideration should solely serve to evaluate, diagnose, or treat the medical need efficiently. Physicians must look not only at one's gender and age, for example, but at all crucial components of who one is in order to better understand the person's situation at hand: race, ancestry, beliefs, current and past illnesses, habits, traumatic events, weight, symptoms, vital signs, and so on. If a patient is viewed as an integrated self in physical care, intersectionality must be just as much, if not more, at the forefront of spiritual or emotional care because these intersecting factors impact the body, the mind, and the spirit. Spiritual caregivers and leaders need to deepen their awareness of intersectionality because it allows them to see the whole person more readily and thus position the caregiver to have greater empathy and understanding of a patient's situation.

If the universe is composed of many beautiful, mysterious, and expanding pieces whose synergy and concurrence sustain the world we know, we can see more clearly the intersection of different factors giving rise to who we are as living creatures. That awareness helps me to approach the other more holistically, whether that is a patient, peer, or staff, and to be more present to them in any given circumstance. Not fully appreciating the interaction of one's realities would neglect one's processing, one's relating, one's barriers and flourishing, and would limit, and perhaps marginalize, the individual created with each of these pieces.

This awareness can be challenging to all of us who grew up in a society that tends to dissect the inseparable parts of a person in order to measure, categorize, and assign value. Single-angled perceptions are the way I, and probably many of us, learned to look at the world, as if an individual feature could define a complex, living, and developing reality. Among many considerations, this meant that in some settings my gender would inform who I was in relation to authorities and leaders, or that my age would limit my ability to be respected in the workplace, or that my birth order would limit the amount of care received by loved ones. Early on and throughout high school, I learned that my role as student in times of a military dictatorship meant that my creativity and critical thinking needed to be repressed until adulthood. Burgeoning societal standards, however, brought new expectations to what it meant, among other features, to be a woman, a student, and a creative being. As my contexts changed, shifts were necessitated, and new learnings were instilled. Furthermore, as I moved to the United States, things that meant something specific in my home country (for example, the advantage of being born in Chile) shifted to almost the opposite within the framework of my current society (being an immigrant in the United States). The color of my skin, my primary language, my faith tradition, and my being born in a prosperous city, which placed me in a powerful position before, now brought a lower status in the new country. Being a person of color in Chile was a category in which I did not belong, yet it is one ascribed to me now in a North American context. Thus, context matters for the consideration of who we are and how we express our identity.

It is a lifelong enterprise to learn that my being in a given circumstance, with all its complexity and multidimensionality, is impacted by the intersection of multiple factors. Such a fascinating and rich journey is only possible with those who model such integration through their own lives, facing multilayered challenges, and consistently honoring the realities that comprise an individual in relation to their environment. My graduate theological studies challenged me to regard myself as a unique composite of many elements that elicit meaning within a given context and to seek such integrity wherever I am, in who I am and who I am becoming. I was valued and accountable for the totality of who I am. This is a hopeful, dignifying, and needed approach that helped me realize my vocation as a chaplain and allows me to continue to grow in perspective and faith. As I am encouraged by this educational approach, I admire the elaborate, harmonious, and rich work of God in the world. Because of intersectionality theory, I was able to be present with a humble heart in the episode I described earlier. I cannot help but bow before the face of God exquisitely present in each individual person.

My experience as a theological student, my history, my religion, my gender, and my race are a few dimensions that form the person I am and that give meaning to my hospital ministry. These components influence my perception and presence in every visit, and being aware of this helps me know myself in relation to others and in relation to their surroundings. I better appreciate the totality of what we bring to each encounter and, in turn, reflect and magnify this reality so it becomes visible to others. When I remind myself of the impact of people's experiences and the meaning of the many aspects of who they are, I think about both my own intersectionality and that of the people within a hospital. Therefore, I am better able to respond with more humaneness and care.

As a chaplain, specifically, I strive to integrate the different elements that make up the beauty and mystery of each individual and situation. This integration brings me closer to others and deepens my connection and compassion toward those who undergo illness, medical emergencies, and pain, as with the man in the emergency room. Our intersectionality is a bridge that helps honor those before us; in doing so, we see better the love, intricacy, and providence of God's handiwork in each of us.

QUESTIONS FOR REFLECTION

1. Paulina Alvarado shares about a hospital experience in her opening memoir story. Have you reflected on a school or work experience where you wondered if the experience would have been different if some part of your identity were different? Reflect and share.
2. What is promising and threatening about identifying and naming our intersectional identities? Those of others?
3. How might your work change if you, and other practitioners in the field, approached your vocation and work through intersectionality theory?

Chapter Sixteen

Bring Your Whole Self through the Door and Let Her Speak

Shaina Williams

"Shaina, you're weird" was not an uncommon statement for me to hear during my childhood. My older siblings would often say this to me as I was growing up. As far back as I can recall, I have always felt "different" and have encompassed a multitude of identities that don't stereotypically go together. I am nearly three decades into my life, and this is becoming increasingly true. I am African American, female, pro-life, vegan, educated, and a Pentecostal/Evangelical Christian. At times, these intersecting identities don't make sense to others: "How can you be black and not eat meat?" "Why would you choose to identify as an Evangelical Christian as a black person?" "How can you be a woman and be antiabortion?" are all variations of questions I have encountered.

As a graduate student in a progressive and predominantly white seminary, I have had a unique experience navigating through readings, assignments, and class discussions in light of my intersecting identities. As I have learned a set of unspoken rules, my "whole self" has often had to evaluate how to participate in a socially appropriate way in this context. This has led to moments of being overwhelmed with the amount of awareness and conscientiousness I feel is required of each part of me, sometimes leading to an internal battle. Over the past four years, I have had to wrestle with the temptation of censoring certain parts of myself to actively participate in assignments and discussions. I ask in some form, "Which part of myself is welcome here? Who in this room might take offense if I am honest? Does my voice even matter?"

If there is one thing I have learned during my theological education, it is that what is seen on the surface is not always true internally. Most of us are far too complicated to fit into the stereotypes that society designates for us. I think about my personal experiences as a black woman and everything I have faced up to this point. To most on the outside looking in, it can appear that minoritized groups are often homogenous. I think of the black community and how we are often perceived as being uneducated, lazy, unreliable, promiscuous, dangerous, poor, and violent. I've also observed that there are many stereotypes regarding how a black person "ought" to act. To some, "acting black" is defined as being boisterous, outspoken, and speaking in Ebonics. To others, it means being in a near constant state of outrage over racial injustice and being led by anger and frustration.

As a black woman, I find the long list of stereotypes and roles associated with the black community to be hurtful and more damaging than I think most realize. These stereotypes have damaged us internally, both in our communities and within ourselves. You see, it is because of these kinds of stereotypes that I was often made fun of and ridiculed by other black children when I was growing up, particularly by other black girls. I've always spoken in a way that many have labeled as "talking white." I've been called "whitewashed" and "Oreo." As a result, I have experienced great anxiety meeting new black people for the first time, fearful that once I speak I will be rejected as not being "black enough."

While things got easier once I graduated from high school and went to college, I still struggled for years with the belief that I was a black reject, one that the black community did not want to claim as their own. These fears intensified once I began my graduate education, and I realized I also failed to fit into the stereotypical mold of the "woke" and educated black person. Thankfully, over the years I have encountered other black people who have had similar fearful experiences of not being the "right" kind of black person. We are not alone in our struggle. A common intersection I have noticed is that, for some, being educated and black is not always viewed as two things that go together. There is a tendency to expect educated black people either to climb the corporate ladder with an elitist attitude or evolve into a fiery civil rights activist. Because of this history, my transition into a contextual education setting primarily made up of women of color was not a seamless one.

After a nine-month internship at an incredible nonprofit that provides basic items for children in need, I needed to secure a second internship for my final year in seminary. As I researched a site our school's director of contextual education recommended, I learned that the organization was in the Central District, the historically black neighborhood in Seattle. Over the last several years, gentrification has affected this neighborhood, causing many people of color to lose their homes and businesses while being edged out of their neighborhood. Through my research, I learned that this organization primarily serves families of color who make 30 to 50 percent of the median income for the area. The majority of the families are single mothers who work to provide a better life for their children. While families in the organization's program are provided with affordable, safe, and clean housing, they are also equipped with an abundance of support and tools to help them move beyond survival into thriving.

I arranged an in-person interview and quickly noticed, upon my arrival, that the majority of those working at the site were black women. What inspired me most was that at the heart of this organization is the belief that people of color are capable and worth more than what society believes. This process involves unlearning the false narratives that have weighed on the black community for far too long. The internship role would help them continue their healing and strengthening work and journey.

I was equally anxious and ecstatic when my internship started. For years, God has given me the deep desire to help empower women and children in need, and I was grateful to be given the opportunity to be of service. While I knew I was placed in a position to directly help women and children for a purpose, I was fearful of how I would be perceived. Old memories as well as imagined fears began to come to the surface of my mind. I was flooded with many fears and uncertainties: What if I attempt to lead this group and the women reject me for how I talk? What if they reject me for my youthful appearance? What if they find me condescending? What if they don't want to share in the group? What if I have nothing to offer them? What if I don't belong here? My supervisors all cautioned me to make sure I established authority over the group and to show up as my "most mature self" since I present as much younger than I actually am. These warnings were repeated several times during the weeks leading up to my group, causing me to have moments of intense doubt. However, amid all these uncertainties, I sought after God and prayed for him to give me the wisdom and strength I needed to effectively help the women. I asked God to give me a focus for the group, one that would get to the souls of the women and bring about healing and restoration. Over time, with God's strength, I continued to push through, and the topics we would focus on as a group would include identity, self-love, and self-respect.

As group sessions began, I quickly realized I was among an incredible group of women who are determined to rise, heal, and overcome. We have much in common and found overlap in what it is like to live in the world as a woman of color.

> We've all experienced the hurt of encountering people who treat us as though we are less valuable, less important, and less authoritative than others.
> We've all been afraid to speak up.
> We've all felt powerless.

We've all felt forgotten and set aside.
We've all wrestled with feeling the need to assimilate and diminish ourselves in certain spaces to make others feel at ease.
We've all been misunderstood.
We've all felt like we have to work extra hard to be considered "almost" equal.
We've all experienced the anguish of feeling mistreated and not always knowing if it's because of the color of our skin.
We've all felt the need to repress our true hurts and frustrations in spaces of work and education.
We've all felt the need to wear different masks and full-fledged uniforms as a means of survival.
We've all been hurt deeply and are trying to find the courage to trust and love.
More than anything, we all want to find healing and feel whole.

I am in awe of how fierce and amazing the women are. While I cannot share specific stories of all that was said during our six-week sessions, I will say that women within this organization have been through heartbreaking circumstances and trauma and are working to build themselves up from the inside out. They have experienced abandonment, loss, unemployment, rejection, abuse, and homelessness. They have fought illnesses, addictions, and countless demons that have done everything in their power to kill, steal, and destroy. But by the grace of God, the women have survived and are determined champions.

A common thread I witnessed in the group was faith and a desire for God. While overt Christian messaging was not allowed, the women, unsolicited, brought Jesus into our conversations, offering what he has done in their lives and sharing about Jesus's love, truth, and wisdom with one another. My heart could not contain the amount of joy I had as their group facilitator witnessing lives and hearts transformed. They are women who want to extinguish destructive generational curses that have been in their families for generations. They are much more complex and aware than many people realize. They are strong, determined, loving, courageous, and authentic. They are working faithfully to overcome every stereotype and barrier the world has thrown at them. They are women of color, mothers, friends, students, wives, workers, preachers, innovators, encouragers, truth tellers, and world changers. Every single one of them rose to the occasion of being their unboxed selves and actively encouraged and lifted one another up. *This*, I realized, is what we need in communities of color and in the world in general.

When I reflect on my experiences in seminary through the lens of my own intersectionality as well as my experiences with the women at my internship, I see that my educational context has done an excellent job inviting students to engage intersectional theory with the hopes of empowering minoritized persons through making room at "the table" and encouraging them to use their voice. We also spend time analyzing subjects through different social and religious traditions, which has given many of us space to share our experiences. My hope concerning intersectionality, both in my specific context and overall, is for theological education to consider that the curriculum is sometimes not as well equipped for certain differences and the combination of those differences in a given context. Some schools are better suited to address certain intersectional identities than others. Though the curriculum often contributes to the flourishing of many students and their becoming, it can also stifle other students' learning when the differences that are important to the student are different than those that are important to the educational institution. So, while intersectional theory is needed, I am reminded through my internship experiences with the women that we must also consider which intersectional identities we are addressing and why.

QUESTIONS FOR REFLECTION

1. Name a time when you negotiated part of your social identity because you felt different from the rest of the group or social norm. What was going on for you, and how did you navigate this difference?
2. Contrarily, identify a time when you felt right at home and comfortable in your intersectional identities, in your seminary community, and/or in your field education experience. How, if at all, did this comfort change your educational experience?
3. What social and intersecting identities are your school and theological field education equipped to name and address? Where do they still need to grow?

Chapter Seventeen

Learning through Our Bodies

Trudy Hawkins Stringer

We still do not know what the body can do.[1]

Learning and teaching that move bodies out of classrooms and into ambiguous spaces, and that expose bodies to the unexpected, challenge normative notions of the construction of knowledge. Engaging experiential pedagogy, theological field education creates new spaces for learning in ways that compel us beyond our cognitive faculty and into a more holistic engagement of multisensory, embodied ways of learning and teaching. In this chapter, we explore the nature and possibilities of embodied learning, examine the resistance to foregrounding bodies in education as well as religion, and explore practices of embodied learning. Using the lenses of theology, educational theory, neuroscience, and lived experience, we will consider inherited traditions and practices in the light of new ways of understanding how we learn and teach.

Perhaps you have heard the famous statement, "I think, therefore I am," one that reverberates with inherited academic, as well as religious, assumptions. While seventeenth-century Enlightenment figure René Descartes and others paved the way for knowledge regarding the human body, the turn to the rational came at a high cost: the splitting of the mind from the body. While this duality of body/mind and body/spirit predates Enlightenment conceptions, these conceptions of corporeality and learning significantly influenced the evolution of learning theory and practice in the Western academic traditions.[2]

Consider an alternate lens on how we learn, that of human infants. What do you notice about the way children learn? For example, when Aden took to his feet, his grandmother named him The Shark, a constantly moving biped exploring his world through oral, tactile, auditory, olfactory, and visual senses, muscle and bone, brain and nerve endings, emotions and intuition. Yes, embodied learning can be risky, such as his fascination with electrical outlets, and sometimes messy, like grape paintings on the wall. And yet, this early "schooling" pervades all cultures. In English we name this "play." Play emerges organically as our initial mode of learning. Play suggests that the full construction of knowledge requires the integration of multiple ways of exploring our world, multiple ways of accumulating data, and multiple ways of constructing knowledge that take us beyond "I think."

Current trends in theological inquiry engage play as important to fully embodied being. Focus on play challenges the sufficiency of rationally grounded pedagogies and engages the body as essential to learning and teaching. Play engages multiple aspects of learning beyond cognitive faculties, including the cerebral cortex, motor cortex, and hypothalamus.[3] In *Growing Down: Theology and Human Nature in the Virtual Age*, Professor Jaco Hamman writes, "It is impossible to imagine a person thriving or flourishing without play being an active part of life."[4] Hamman also notes that play "can undo past formations, including trauma, and open future possibilities."[5] Note that research on pedagogies of play have largely focused on children and youth, as if the body disappears in adult learning.

Now consider your educational experiences. How have you experienced your body in classrooms? When did you experience your body invited into a classroom as essential to learning? Some of us remember desks in linear rows designed to contain bodies so as not to distract from learning, or lecture halls with desks bolted to the floor, holding bodies in place, facing forward so as not to disturb thinking. Others may remember more open classrooms where bodies were invited to move and explore. Consider Maria Montessori's development of embodied pedagogical practices over 100 years ago.[6] There are myriads of ways that bodies are edited out of and invited into how we learn. Cultivating awareness of our bodies in academia invites deeper understanding of our ways of learning and teaching—and may feel uncomfortable to those of us steeped in traditional Western pedagogical practices.

Reflecting on her journey as student and professor of sociology, Becky Thompson writes, "I realized that I was passing on to my students some of the costs I paid to become an academic. . . . I begin to realize that the academy asked people to trade in their body parts, anything below the neck, in order to be successful. I remember feeling like I had ransomed off all my body parts, except my head, in order to finish the book."[7] Thompson urges us to consider the hidden costs of disembodied learning and teaching and, as we will see later, possibilities for embodied learning and teaching, including the curious terminology of *tenderness* as a needed pedagogical practice.[8]

Before returning to our learning roots, engaging advances in what we know about the brain-body interconnectedness, and risking a foray into a pedagogy of tenderness, let's pause to briefly explore the troubled histories of bodies in academic and religious institutions.

TROUBLED HISTORY OF BODIES

When our bodies become objects of fear and sites of sinfulness, what is lost?

To more fully understand the trajectories of disembodiment, consider the histories of bodies in the intertwined institutions of academia and religion. While I write from a white, cisgendered, temporarily able-bodied, Western, Christian, Protestant, mainline context and a university-based divinity school theological field education department located in the southern United States, the questions raised by these histories emerge in multiple faith traditions and academic contexts. I encourage you to consider your particular religious and academic historical contexts, the articulated and implicit attitudes toward bodies, and how these attitudes shape our academic and religious practices of teaching and learning.

In *Enfleshing Freedom: Body, Race, and Being*, Catholic theologian M. Shawn Copeland confronts "somatophobia":

> The ambivalence with which Christian thought focuses on the sex of the matter may be traced to a persistent *somatophobia* or fear of flesh. This fear stems from a conceptual axis that compounds both distortions of Neoplatonism, with its tendency to idealism, suspicion of ambiguity, and discomfort with matter, *and* Pauline and Augustinian warnings about flesh and its pleasures.[9]

Listen as Copeland paints a history of disembodiment that sounds strangely familiar to contemporary Western ears. Reflect for a moment on when you have encountered, in yourself and/or others, idealization (perfectionism),[10] resistance to engaging the uncertainly of ambiguity, discomfort with the messiness of matter, and diminution of the enfleshed human body. Somatophobia deprives us of the fullness of our being in the world and truncates our knowing of the self, the holy, the other, and creation.

In *Poetics of the Flesh*, professor of religion and Latinx studies Mayra Rivera writes, "But flesh has ambiguous connotations. Indeed, its materiality often carries the weight of sin."[11] Rivera describes in detail the ways that flesh, in Christian traditions, has become the "site of sin" and left us relying on the limited lens of cognition, resulting in distorted theological anthropologies and cultural systems. Rivera observes that these negative valuations of flesh largely connote female flesh.[12] Rivera writes,

> Flesh is an ambivalent term that names a rather slippery materiality. . . . Flesh is always becoming. Air, water, food, sunlight, and even societies of microorganisms enter our bodies to weave the delicate tissue of our flesh. Impercept-

ibly to the naked eye, cell by cell, day after day, the world constitutes your body and mine. And our bodies enter into the constitution of the world. They are intimately our own, singular and irreplaceable, and yet formed by and given to the world.[13]

Copeland and Rivera offer a vision of enfleshed, ever-changing bodies, always in process, always finite. Perhaps our fear of nonbeing, our fear of losing the illusion of control, fuels the editing of unpredictable, messy, finite bodies out of spaces of learning and worship.

Not only are bodies connected to sin in certain strains of Christian traditions and diminished in traditional pedagogical practices; these and other traditions can sanction systems of oppression enacted on certain bodies. In the United States, we see the fruits of continuing oppression in the need for Black Lives Matter, a twenty-first-century continuation of resistance to the enslavement of black bodies and its morphing into Jim Crow oppression, then the cradle-to-prison pipeline[14]; in Native populations' call for justice in the face of a history of Native genocide; in the border detention of brown bodies, seeking asylum, fleeing violence, hunger, and risking death in hopes of a better life; in the Me Too movement, another chapter in the long history of the struggle to free women's bodies toward full participation in all aspects of human community; in movements resisting the oppression of LGBTQI+ bodies; in movements calling us to awareness of other-abled bodies. While this is by no means a comprehensive listing of oppressions enacted on particular types of bodies, it is suggestive of the importance of cultivating body awareness, creating embodied pedagogies, developing critical consciousness of systems, and inviting all bodies into classrooms, into seats of power, and into places of worship. It is also a reminder of the richness of diversity in creation itself.

BEYOND MIND/BODY DUALITY

> If the construction of knowledge is confined solely to our cognitive faculties, what is lost?

Returning to our early learning roots combined with engaging advances in what we know about the brain-body interconnectedness suggest possibilities beyond the mind/body dichotomy and toward an integrated understanding of, as one student wrote, "mindbodyspirit," engaging the fullness of being in learning and teaching.[15]

Early-twentieth-century philosopher and mathematician Alfred North Whitehead challenged the bifurcation of mind and body with prescient insights predating the emergence of the discipline of neuroscience. In *Let the Bones Dance: Embodiment and the Body of Christ*, theologian and minister

Marcia Mount Shoop engages Whitehead's conception of feeling "a complex and uncommonly used theological category . . . not simply experience; rather . . . the physical mode of experience that grounds, conditions, and gives life to all our experiences."[16]

Feeling, Shoop continues, is "constantly becoming part of our inheritance as data that translate into every part of us. It is the fabric, the thread, and the seamstress of who we are . . . [P]hysical and mental types of experience are not in opposition or clearly distinct from one another."[17]

Pause for a moment and remember Aden, The Shark, the early embodied learner. Was he not enacting "the physical mode of experience that grounds, conditions, and gives life to all our experiences"?

In the introduction to *Learning Bodies*, Danish educators and editors Juelskjaer, Moser, and Schilhab write, "Whether we are dealing with such many-sided issues as neurological foundations of learning processes, skill acquisition, mental health and illness, aesthetics or physical space where learning is going on, you never will get to the complexity of 'the matter' unless you keep the body in mind."[18]

They remark on the early-twenty-first-century growth of "knowledge and interdisciplinary dialogue in the research fields of 'learning' and 'body.'" Examples of such interest appear in the disciplines of sociology, feminist research, medical anthropology, and "new interdisciplinary approaches . . . between . . . neurosciences, psychology and philosophy, especially phenomenology."[19]

From a framework of phenomenology and movement theory, Professor Karen Barbour in the University of Waikato Faculty of Education, New Zealand, writes persuasively regarding the place of the body in human knowing:

> Integral to lived experience is the notion of the "lived body": a non-dualistic understanding of the conscious, intentional, and unified body, soul and mind in action in the world. Affected by dominant Western culture's denial and repression of the body, and of experience as a source of knowledge, lived movement experience has only recently been studied academically.[20]

University of Kentucky gender and women's studies professor Susan Bordo explores the long trajectory of diminution of bodies in Western philosophical history and reminds us that, without the hard work required to change deeply embedded systems, awareness is not enough: "What remains the constant . . . is the construction of body as something apart from the true self. . . . That which is not body is the highest, the best, the noblest, the closest to God; that which is body is the albatross, the heavy drag on self-realization."[21] Bordo goes on to explain the necessity of systemic change:

> Clearly, then, mind/body dualism is no mere philosophical position, to be defended or dispensed with by clever argument. Rather, it is a practical metaphysics that has been deployed and socially embodied in medicine, law, literary and artistic representations, the psychological construction of self, interpersonal relationships, popular culture, and advertisements—a metaphysics which will be deconstructed only through concrete transformation of the institutions and practices that sustain it.[22]

Whitehead, Mount Shoop, Moser, Schilhab, Barbour, and Bordo's insights resonate with claims of culturally embedded mind/body dualisms, so deeply embedded that we fail to see what is before us—and more importantly within us.[23] These authors from diverse disciplines invite us to don new lenses and consider deeply what is lost when bodies are edited out of the classroom.

EMBODIED LEARNING AND TEACHING

> When enfleshed bodies reclaim their place in learning and teaching, what is gained?

What are practices of embodied learning and teaching, and how do we go about cultivating them? What does embodiment ask us to risk? Perhaps you are already finding ways of embodying your learning, your teaching, preaching, and caregiving. In this section we explore one professor's journey toward embodied teaching and learning. Becky Thompson, professor of sociology, in *Teaching with Tenderness: Towards an Embodied Practice*, writes, "Beginning to understand the centrality of the body in the classroom came from realizing somewhere . . . in my academic training . . . I had left my body . . . I wanted it back . . . My . . . process has helped me see how students who are in their bodies often tell us much more than what they say."[24]

Thompson's work also speaks to the strained temper of the current culture, nationally and globally, and its impact in academic contexts, particularly those contexts engaging issues of suffering, healing, and justice in course content. Thompson's categories resonate not only with issues we engage in theological education; they show up live in the bodies in our classrooms and learning contexts. This is why we can no longer afford the cost of editing our flesh, our bodies, out of learning and teaching. Addressing U.S. academic culture, Thompson points out, "Prior to the 1960s, the academy was primarily monotribal (the white tribe) . . . shar[ing] symbols, morals, and assumptions that reinforced the mind body split and a rationalized system of education. . . . Nowadays, more of us teach in multitribal classrooms."[25]

To inform embodied practice, Thompson takes an interdisciplinary approach, drawing from three areas of study: multiracial feminist pedagogy, contemplative practices, and trauma studies. Multiracial feminist pedagogies offer both an antidote to exclusionary aspects of white feminism and acknowledge the entanglements of gender and race/ethnicity in bodies.[26] Advances in brain imaging technologies offer clues to how contemplative practices influence embodied brain function.[27] Trauma studies "offer insight into how the human mind and body react to living through trauma and witnessing trauma or both."[28] Trauma-informed pedagogy guides practices that acknowledge that we learn through embodied experiences and that embodied experiences travel with us into spaces of learning and teaching.[29] Trauma-informed pedagogy involves the risk of engaging memories embedded in bodies, hurt as well as healing, pain as well as pleasure, cruelty as well as care. How much more do we risk by removing bodies, our own and yours, from learning and teaching?

Thompson risks proposing a pedagogy of tenderness defined as

> those spontaneous, planned, and found rituals of inclusion that lean us towards justice, that rest on rigorous study, that treat the classroom as sacred space, that coach each other into habits of deep listening, that treat memory as an antidote to alienation, that multiply joy.[30] . . . I imagine a pedagogy of tenderness that is part mindfulness, part playfulness, part intuition, part analysis.[31]

Note that Thompson finds tenderness and rigorous study not at odds but as partners in embodied pedagogy, "a body centered approach to teaching, one that keeps the intellect in the room while teaching through the body."[32] Thompson highlights embodied pedagogical practices, engaging contemplative practices (mindfulness, meditation, yoga), attention to movement in the classroom, intentional engagement of space, ritual practices of "Who am I?" and "loving kindness," collaborative and embodied writing assignments, naming rituals (from Rev. Dr. Katie Cannon), gathering in circles, ritualizing eye contact, deep listening, theater, symbolic objects, playlist creation, and closing rituals, to name a few.[33]

Over time I have experimented with practices designed to keep "the intellect in the room while teaching through the body" and to keep the body in mind while engaging experiential pedagogy in their respective learning contexts.[34] These are pedagogical practices I find invite the body into learning.

Give attention to space and bodies by assessing and altering the teaching-learning space to encourage forming a community capable of listening deeply as well as imagining alternative spaces in which to gather.[35]

Consider these examples of opening rituals that build learning community:

- An elemental ritual attending to breath and breathing deeply together, slowing down, noticing, listening to one's body in community with others to bring the scattered self into fuller presence.
- An invitational space for naming what you—and teachers—are needful of acknowledging in order to experience being fully present to one another.[36]
- Sharing narratives of personal journeys leading to theological education, including an invitation to consider attendant visual, auditory, tactile, taste, and olfactory presentations symbolic of the journey.
- Being present to food, pausing to attend to smell, sound, shape, texture, and taste of familiar foods eaten with attention to sensory knowing. Sharing favorite foods becomes a sensory communal ritual connected to deep memories. Meeting at the table becomes a ritual of cooking and sharing a meal.
- Moving outdoors, walking around campus, not to "get somewhere" but to notice nature using your sensory capacities. Eating and moving outdoors become not means to an end but practices of body awareness.

Case study methodology invites your reflection on inner embodied awareness while engaging critical consciousness relative to issues of justice and cultural systems and rigorous theological reflection as necessary components for generative ministry practice.

Context analysis assignments invite you to turn to your body and senses—asking what smells, tastes, sounds, visuals, and touch you experience in the context. Giving time and space to move bodies and rearrange space to form in small theological discussion groups subtly invites bodies into the classroom with opportunities to "see each other's eye."[37]

Mapping your discussions on a whiteboard gives visual expression to theological insights expressed in both words and drawings while inviting your body to move and claim agency in the classroom.

These are but a few of many ways of inviting bodies into learning and teaching. Which do you find inviting your body's full participation?

Learning that interweaves rigorous study and tenderness requires imagination, collaboration, and risk. At best, these practices build trust that allows bodies to show up, allows us to know and be known—to see into one another's eyes and to learn with our bodies in mind, to learn from what does and does not work, lessening the competition of success/failure binaries and the pathology of perfection.

Embodied practice is "a pedagogy that works inside and outside the classroom."[38] What could be more resonant with the learning and teaching in theological field education? Experiential pedagogy insists that we move back and forth, creating a dance between classroom and congregations, hospitals, prisons, movement building, domestic violence shelters, campus ministries, immigrant and refugee advocacy programs, and the list goes on; we weave a praxis tapestry of embodied theology and practice in continual conversation, challenging and informing one another, lamenting and celebrating, elaborating ever-changing patterns of our embodied journeying—moving, breathing, learning together with all our senses, in community, sharing in diverse, finite, enfleshed being.

QUESTIONS FOR REFLECTION

1. What is your relationship with your body?
2. Consider your particular religious and academic contexts, their history, inherited theologies, and their articulated and implicit attitudes toward bodies. How do these shape your academic and religious practices of teaching and learning?

SUGGESTED READING

Mayra Rivera, *Poetics of the Flesh* (Durham, NC: Duke University Press, 2015).

Marcia Mount Shoop, *Let the Bones Dance: Embodiment and the Body of Christ* (Louisville, KY: Westminster John Knox, 2010).

Becky Thompson, *Teaching with Tenderness: Toward an Embodied Practice* (Urbana: University of Illinois Press, 2017).

Chapter Eighteen

Cultivating the Mood to Linger

Angela Denise Davis

> All travelers, somewhere along the way, find it necessary to check their course, to see how they are doing. We wait until we are sick, or shocked into stillness, before we do the commonplace thing of getting our bearings. And yet, we wonder why we are depressed, why we are unhappy, why we lose our friends, why we are ill-tempered. This condition we pass on to our children, our husbands, our wives, our associates, our friends. Cultivate the mood to linger. . . . Who knows? God may whisper to you in the quietness what [God] has been trying to say to you, oh, for so long a time.
> —Howard Thurman, *Deep Is the Hunger*

The line between "before" and "after" is not thin. It is not the invisible line that separates two photographs portraying a body that has undergone drastic weight loss. Rather, it is the river's stretch that divides two banks from one another. Although "after" may start at the bank of the other shore, it is not a static landing. Each footstep forward is a walk on dynamic territory. You can never go back to the land of before, just as you can't step into the same river twice; everything is new after a loss of some sort. It may be weight, ability, relationship, income, or country. In the land of "after," you are always offered the opportunity of awe and the probability of anguish.

I often talk about my life as before blindness and after blindness. Of course, this often reduces the rolling waters of my vision loss to a simplicity that it never had. The muddy, murky waters of transitioning into life as a newly blind person were complicated. One thing is constant, though. I always start my story recounting my time in Namibia.

Namibia will always be the landmark where my feet left the bank of "before." It was the last place where I saw the world in technocolor. I have never forgotten what it was like when our group of theological educators and students arrived in Namibia for a two-week travel field experiential class in the summer of 2003. The sky over the outskirts of Windhoek, Namibia, was strangely familiar. The land was flat. It was not a stretch for me to think about my native home, Wichita, Kansas. At night, the stars were all the same, and there were so many, like the stars I watched while sitting on my front porch as a teenager. I was so ready to leave home then, so ready to be someplace else. Here I was in southern Africa. I knew I was not in Kansas anymore, but this country of a million stars felt like home.

During the trip, I would come out as a lesbian to my colleague, navigate a query by a queer student who tried to out me, and listen to a butch African lesbian recount her story to our group. It all seemed too emotionally charged, but I refused to allow my body to linger with what any of it meant. I swallowed moments of pain even as I gloried in the beauty of Namibia's landscape and people. The pink flamingos on the beach, sand dunes that were impossible for me to climb, and the generosity of our driver, Passat, who translated one of Oliver Mtukudzi's songs that bespoke the devastating reality of the HIV/AIDS crisis in Zimbabwe. The song, "Todii—What Shall We Do," sounded happy to our American ears until the lyrics were unveiled.

We spent two weeks in Namibia and then returned to Nashville, Tennessee, where I was the admissions director at Vanderbilt Divinity School. Then "after" came very quickly. Three months after my return, I began losing vision in my left eye. It was a week before Thanksgiving. The diagnosis was optic neuritis. A week later, I developed intermittent swells of heat in my left leg and was given a prescription for Neurontin. My body had a bad interaction with the drug, and I was left unable to eat any food or drink any liquids for eight weeks. The swift current of change was dragging me down a river of uncertainty. When I queried my neurologist and neuro opthamologist about my prognosis, they could only say things were "highly variable." I was legally blind by the end of that January and would have a total of six optic neuritis occurrences by June.

The vision loss was accompanied by various health issues that only complicated my road to blind rehabilitation. I was in and out of the hospital, with one memorable time in particular. It was early morning, and the Vanderbilt Medical Center hospital room was dark and quiet. During those days, time lingered, and the silence was plentiful. I was awake, and in the stillness of the early morning, a knowing came out of my body. It wasn't an audible voice, but I heard every word. It said, "After all that has happened, you should have lost your mind, but you've got a peace that no one understands."

It was true; my life seemed to be falling apart, but at the same time, it seemed as if something fantastic was happening. By fantastic I mean imaginary; it didn't seem to be my life, and, therefore, I found things quite interesting. In the early months of my blindness, I was forced to "cultivate a mood to linger," as the mystic Howard Thurman would say. My fast-paced world before vision loss did not hold much space for such a slowdown in pace. I learned to take life moment by moment as I acquired new information to help me live in my "new normal." I had to trust that my body would lead the way in my learning.

It would be years before I fully understood how my body had changed to offer me a more secure place in the world. What I did not know initially was that my gait had widened to accommodate my search for equilibrium. My hearing became even more crucial as I navigated sidewalks and hallways. I learned more by touching a thing than seeing it with my damaged optic nerves. I could no longer rely on my eyes to gauge another person's body language. I had to listen for it. The uneasy silence of friends and acquaintances who were reintroduced to the new blind me was a dead giveaway regarding their discomfort. Touch and tone were more important to me in communication than what I could physically see. Where I would have been able to judge an interaction by the visage of the approaching person, now I had to quickly assess who was standing at my side.

Of course, I was not the only one who was learning how to travel this new landscape. I was acutely aware of how my presence in the workplace created space for conversation. Although it was never determined that my trip to Namibia was the cause of my vision loss, I knew that some in the administration thought it was possible that I had contracted something that attacked my optic nerves. I also believed this, and I still do. We were trying to figure out where to go next in this journey, and I will always be grateful for the empathy I received even though we were quite clueless about how to go forward.

It was a vulnerable time trying to find my way in the workplace without any rehabilitation and under the watchful eyes of the administration, faculty, and students. I often felt as if I were naked at a cocktail party with fully clothed people. I will never forget preaching my first sermon as a blind clergyperson. It was for a chapel service at the school. I took my shoebox-sized CCT reader to the podium and tried to read each line of greatly magnified text. It was excruciating. Shortly after that experience, I decided to leave my position as the admissions director and was offered a part-time position assisting the academic dean with special projects for the next year.

As my body was teaching me about living as a blind person, I was painfully aware that most good-intentioned people around me did not understand my world. I chalked up some comments as being clumsy instead of being cruel. One professor, in a casual conversation with me and one of his colleagues, said that "we all would be disabled at some point." His conflation of aging with a disability was problematic, but more importantly, I felt as if he didn't recognize the person standing in front of him. It was not a possible future of disability I was grappling with but a very present profound loss of vision. His words seemed like a dismissal of my body's current battle.

It was harder to deal with how "church folk" regarded disability and my blindness, though. I can recall my pastor preaching a sermon where he mentioned that "God was not disabled." I did not hear any other words he spoke after that. I indulged religious people who either thought this was the work of the Devil tempting me or the work of God empowering me. The most heart-rending reasoning, though, was my mother's assessment that my blindness was caused by acceptance of my sexual orientation. I was not out to everyone at the time, but I quickly learned that I could not be in the closet and blind. I made a calculated move to honor all the ways my body was teaching me how to be me. I also rooted myself in my understanding that my vision loss was not the work of God or the Devil. It was a swift transition in the current of my life. The blind me, black me, woman me, and lesbian me had to learn to sink or swim.

At the time, I was working with a therapist who encouraged me to get outside the safety of my apartment. It was a tall order considering that I was afraid of crossing streets and had been instructed in only the most basic white cane techniques. Initially, I would leave my apartment and walk to the end of the street only to be mocked by the intersection that I was too afraid to cross. I was receiving services from the vocational rehabilitation agency in Nashville, but it was not comprehensive. An opportunity for me to train at a National Federation of the Blind rehabilitation center in Minneapolis, Minnesota, offered me the freedom to travel that my therapist had encouraged.

BLIND (Blindness Learning In New Dimensions), Inc. changed my life. I spent 10 months learning how to put the pieces of me back together. What made BLIND, Inc., different from so many blind rehab centers was that we had to train in sleep shades as if we had no vision at all. The theory was that we would learn to trust our senses more and not rely on residual vision. I know that if it had not been for that training, my life would be very different now.

I learned how to cook for myself and groups of up to 40. Until that time, I lived off peanut butter sandwiches, cereal, and on fancier days spaghetti. I learned to operate power tools like saws, drills, and sanders in the woodshop. I still have all my fingers. I learned how to read braille and train my ears for the synthetic voices that live in my computer and smartphone. It was no surprise, though, that of all the things I learned at BLIND, Inc., the most important was how to cross streets.

Orientation and mobility is a fundamental training that allows blind individuals to learn how to orient in space and move around in it. The possession of a white cane is useless unless one knows how to use it. The center's orientation and mobility training included a series of drop-offs where the student would be taken to various locations in Minneapolis and then instructed to find the route back to the center on his or her own. The drop-offs were increasingly difficult, and the culmination of the training was a final graduation walk of some difficulty.

My final walk is quite memorable. I can still recall the day I stood on a bridge in Minneapolis looking down at the Mississippi. The river has such a sweet invitation. I was in the middle of my graduation walk. I took off my sleep shades, which we had to wear, and watched the flow of water beneath me. The river was going somewhere. It was moving. Hope is what helps you get across the bridge of the Mississippi, the Jordan, or any other river in life's journey. For an instant, I thought about what it would be like to find myself in the swirl of those currents below. I put my sleep shades back on and declined the river's invitation.

I can imagine that many residents of Minneapolis find it odd and dangerous for blind people to walk the city in sleep shades. The idea of trusting the body in that way may be difficult for many to appreciate. The experience was empowering for me, and it informed the way I moved in all areas of my life, not just on slabs of concrete and asphalt but in the deep interior landscape of my soul.

There is a lot we can learn from the way blind people travel in the world. A blind person standing still at the corner of an intersection is not necessarily lost. We so often judge the inactivity of someone or something because we don't perceive them to be moving. Our fast-paced world does not always allow for the appreciation of stillness. There is often the assumption that if one is not moving then one is not active, but stillness is not void of action. The act of lingering at a traffic light has the same power as lingering in life. It is the act of getting information about one's present space and direction for moving forward.

There have been incidents where folks assume I am lost at the intersection and they either pull me into the street to cross with them or tell me that it is safe to cross. One of the first things I learned in orientation and mobility was the danger of trusting someone's footsteps instead of my ears. My indication to cross is not when I hear others cross or when I am told by someone else that the coast is clear. I have to listen to my own body reading the flow of traffic. I have to gather stillness, trust my gut, and move forward. This wisdom holds true for a city street or even a difficult conversation.

There have been seasons in my life when I have felt it necessary to linger in the moment as my life was approaching an intersection and, as in my orientation and mobility training, I had to first be still in order to orient myself and to understand where I was located and sense what was around me. One must be still at these points in life because there are many things that can misinform you. Even some things that are designed to be helpful, like audible traffic signals, can be misleading if you don't know which chirp represents safe passage for which street. It is important at those junctures to linger even longer than usual.

In the land of my "after," I am still learning and revisiting things about how to be blind. In 2017, I moved to San Francisco to work at the Lighthouse for the Blind. One day, I was injured on the BART, the city's rail system. I tore the meniscus on both sides of my left knee. The physical therapist assigned to my case noticed that I walked with a wide gait. She told me that this is not uncommon for a lot of blind individuals. It is an attempt to gain equilibrium, but it actually has a negative effect on the body. I now mind the width of my gait when walking, and I stand in awe of how my body continually offers ways of learning how to adjust to the world after trauma, injury, or estrangement. If we listen, we can learn.

In theory, I suppose there is a difference between the "before blindness" and "after blindness" Angela. I see my loss of vision as being a distillation of myself. It funneled me through limitations that have provided structure for my true self to grow and recognize that the most important location in my life is "now."

Chapter Nineteen

The Mystery of Embodiment and Friendship

Allison Waters

It's a cold evening in February. I'm exhausted—really exhausted, in every sense of the word. In fact, I am debilitated in body, mind, and soul. I am a social worker and spent my day talking to women with intellectual/developmental disabilities about their experiences of sexual assault and manipulation. I spoke to an angry, hurting mother about the discrimination and isolation the social services system has inflicted on her son with autism. My day illuminated the harsh realities of scarcity, trauma, and injustice in the world. All of this was the forefront of my day, while in the background I'm missing my family who is far away. I'm worried about paying bills. I'm struggling to take care of myself in the midst of taking care of others. At any moment, I feel like I could fall to the floor in a puddle of anxiety and despair.

There is still two hours left in this day. I am in a room with 80 bodies scurrying around me filled with joy and trauma, stress and relief, anxiety and enthusiasm. It's our weekly evening gathering, where people with and without intellectual disabilities come to eat together, be themselves, and make friends. I began volunteering here at Reality Ministries when I started graduate school. It was a refuge from my academic, competitive life, a place I could simply be myself and enter this conglomeration of vulnerability and humanness. Now, I work here, and it doesn't always feel like a refuge. Especially today, because today I've given myself completely to this place and have been left completely depleted. But these 80 scrambling bodies don't know what I'm going through. Everywhere I turn there is another person wanting to talk or wanting my cheery affection. Everywhere I turn there is a person with a problem they want me to fix or a stress they want me to soothe. Even when I turn to walk away, there is a person coming up behind me, grabbing my sides, poking me and squealing in my ear with delight. Eighty bodies pressing in on me, and I begin to wonder how much more I can take.

But in a moment of divine intervention, the crowd clears, and I see Jack across the room.

He's in the corner, looking at the wall, rocking back and forth with his hands flapping at his sides. His hair is curly, his eyes kind. I can hear that grumbling, sighing noise that he makes, even from far away. It's a nice sound. The tenor of it is not panicked or expectant, just a signal that he is there, participating in this community. I desperately rush to him, and my body collapses in the seat next to him. He shifts his body a little to rock toward me, acknowledging my presence, and grumbles a little under his breath. I feel the comfort of being with an old friend protecting me from the crowd. "Hi, Jack," I say, and he continues to rock. He is quiet, except his low humming. He holds his hand out, and I squeeze it. It is a more intimate communication than I've received all day. It says to me, "I'm here, you're here, and that's enough." Through the rest of the programming, I just sit with him, being in his presence. He rocks and hums, and holds my hands, and I am able to rest. There is no expectation to resort to words. No expectation that I need to solve his problems, fix anything, or even give him affection. I can simply be there and find rest in being together.

We, as a society, have taught and absorbed that friendship is only for people who can intellectually ascend to meet one another, have similar interests, have deep conversations, participate in the same activities, and do nice things for each other. It is easy to act from the implicit belief that people like Jack, who are most often characterized by words like "autism" and "nonverbal," cannot participate in the basic human function of friendship. And yet, Jack provides me with a type of deep friendship that is unique: rest from expectations. The most fundamental thing I need from my friends is for them to acknowledge that I am there, and that is enough.

Jack's way of being fulfills this fundamental need at the forefront of our time together. It does not get swept up in small talk or planning time to see each other or talking about what is happening in our lives. His friendship holds me, heals me, and is constantly revealing more to me. Here in this moment, I am learning, once again, a deeper meaning of friendship.

So much of mainstream acceptable forms of communication rely on verbal and written forms of language. When a person does not participate in such, they are inevitably left out of discussions, connections, and friendships. Part of this is simply that society is so rigid about communication that people literally do not know how to embody other forms of communication when talking is not an option. It is a long, slow process to unlearn this impulse and let go of our need for talking to connect with one another. This most often begins with teachers of embodied languages.

At Reality Ministries, we embody many types of communication. We are a shuffling, bustling mass of bodies speaking. So many different shapes, sizes, and colors of bodies, bustling around each other. Lots of hugs, pinches, kisses, poking, tickling, humming, singing, patting, squeezing. So many bodies together. When I first started coming to Reality, I was so happy for all these bodies smashing and crashing into each other. It was material and real. I was learning to use my entire body to receive and give connection, communication, and friendship.

It took me a while to learn to appreciate friendships with people like Jack that necessarily exist beyond the bounds of verbal communication, because my rigid implicit beliefs about what it means to be friends made the silence awkward. I avoided people I couldn't talk to because I didn't know how to exist without performing the act of friendship in a particular way. I was very comfortable with the idea that I could accept these people for exactly who they were, accept their "disability" and offer them my performance, but it never explicitly occurred to me, in the beginning, that perhaps what they were offering me was a chance to step off this exhausting stage so I could confront all these rigid beliefs and receive another way of friendship, one that did not rely on verbal communication.

We often cannot name why we act, believe, or feel the way we do. Our unexamined and deeply ingrained values are not often taught using logic and rationale but through the embodied languages of community and relationships. Our bodies hold so much wisdom, often revealed to us through immeasurable things like love, hope, faith, and joy. When we interact with a person or community that confronts our ingrained values, our souls churn; it can feel like awkwardness and discomfort, or delight and curiosity. What is happening cannot necessarily be explained in academic terms because it is the body's wisdom swelling and growing, revealing something new to us.

As I sit with Jack, a beautiful lesson begins to unfold within me once again. He is not teaching me something through words or a logical argument. With his hand reaching out to mine, his steady presence, and the rhythm of his body rocking back and forth, he is teaching me that friendship is not an achievement or performance but a deep recognition between souls. This is the mystery of embodied learning.

Chapter Twenty

Breathing into Being

Affirming the Enfleshed Transgender and Gender-Queer Imago Dei

Damien Pascal Domenack

It was the transgender and gender-queer (TGQ) affinity group I facilitated in the university LGBTQI+ center, where I had been the graduate student worker for the past year, that led me to choose the site as my field education placement. This placement allowed me to administer queer pastoral care by caring for the needs of LGBTQI+ students. Religion is a sensitive topic in the transgender community, especially among the 18- to 25-year-old students who are exploring gender fluidity and/or medically transitioning. As a transmasculine-identified person with the privilege of passing, I make sure to talk about my gender as fluid even though it appears fixed. The Bible is weaponized to justify theologies that are divisive and toxic to the whole body of God by supporting the marginalization and criminalization of the transgender, nonbinary, and gender-queer community. Members of our TGQ community (including myself) are directly impacted by violent theologies that encourage families to reject LGBTQI+ people if they come out. I expected to code theological language because of the embodied religious trauma within the center itself. My office hours were spent conducting mentoring/counseling sessions, mediations, and accountability processes, and facilitating TGQ.

Within the immigrant, social justice, trans and gender-queer communities that formed me, I managed to find the warm feel of church, that special sense of belonging. My goal was to build brave new spaces for community with the members of TGQ to be present in while witnessing and embracing our whole selves as worthy of belonging in beloved community. During TGQ we would mostly spend the hour together talking about our shared trans identities, trans-cestors, starting hormones, trans politics, chest binding, dysphoria, shame, regret, high pain tolerance, top surgery fund-raisers, and navigating romantic relationships. Out of the 10 affinity groups, TGQ was the only one that met on a weekly basis due to the emotional impact faced by members in our university and local community. The one key person that pushed for weekly meetings when I first started facilitating the group showed up every single week. At times it was just them and I, and we would still meet. After a few weeks of learning how I facilitate, they accepted my offer to cofacilitate TGQ with me. My underlying goal was to foster and support the courage and resilience of the group in hopes that TGQ would extend beyond the center and to the surrounding community. By the end of the second semester, the group decided to move to meeting twice a month. Through trust-building exercises and TGQ dinner takeovers at local food spots, folx created brave spaces together outside of the center.

TGQ decided to meet during fall break since the majority of our community who live on campus do not go home during the break because their families are not welcoming of their identities. I sensed my cofacilitators' anxiety throughout the prep for TGQ. I reminded them of our simple purpose of holding space for the conversations folx bring with them. Group began with stating the intentionality of the space and our shared identity, then introductions (name, pronouns used in group and outside of our group), and the icebreaker, "name the song you cannot get out of your head this week." As we made our go-around of introductions, I quickly assessed the room and realized we were a group of nine transmasculine-spectrum (he/they/them/theirs) folx. I sat there wondering for a moment about the trans women who were part of the group last year. I briefly drifted into imagining a strategic conversation with them: "How was your fall break? Did you go home for fall break? No wonder we didn't see you at TGQ! Do you have any suggestions or ideas of what you would like from TGQ this year?" After our introductions and the icebreaker, I turned the focus over to the group. Someone shared a story about a professor casually asking, "What's your birth name?" to which the student responded, "I am not comfortable sharing that information with you," and was able to walk away without feeling shamed. The student expressed that their confidence allowed them to have a voice in that moment thanks to the practice sessions we have in TGQ. We then transitioned to a quick "best practices" go-around of how to navigate uncomfortable questions. There was a positive shift in the room after that, and folx shared online resources as they expressed their challenges in communicating their fluidity to cisheteronormative classmates and family members.

As our time began to wind down, I assessed the physical comfort in the space by paying close attention to how people were holding themselves and realized I was the only person who was not wearing a compression chest binder. Throughout TGQ I had realized I was the only person sitting comfortably and felt the visceral discomfort of our group members. They sat with hunched shoulders, unable to take a deep full breath as they constantly adjusted themselves in their seats while engaging in dialogue. I was transported to a time when I would attend groups like TGQ where my community was made up of trans and gender-nonconforming people of color and transmasculine-spectrum folx. I came into my transmasculine identity with older trans women of color in New York City. TGQ is the complete opposite of those spaces, and yet the need for community and trust gained in dialogue is just as great.

I was hesitant to lead a breathing meditation because I knew I needed to breathe and wanted to test the spiritual waters. When I asked, "Would you all like me to lead you in a 10-minute breathing meditation at the end of group, or hold a quiet self-directed breathing meditation, or no mediation? All are welcome, just let me know." They all replied with a succinct "yes." I led them through a breathing exercise and offered these words to close: "As you breathe into your core and feel the strength of your breath, may you feel the power of this community supporting you through the challenges you choose to take on. May you feel the strength of your breath and trust that it will carry your voice as you take on those challenges." When folx opened their eyes, they expressed gratitude for that moment of collective vulnerability in an all-transmasculine space. It was in that moment that I faced my privilege as a trans person who "passes" as male and no longer wears a chest binder.

Sitting with this group, I felt both the visceral discomfort of having been bound for five years and the injustice of having worked three jobs for five years to earn the $8,000 to pay for a surgery to affirm my life. Instead of sharing this normative statement about me, I chose to lift up the diverse experiences within my formative trans community by reminding the group that there are folx who choose not to have the medical industrial complex dictate their gender and do not undergo surgery or take hormones. I realized I too needed to breathe into this tension. When I asked folx about meditating, it came from a place of spiritual privilege, since I have training, access, and resources to lead contemplative practices throughout the week at divinity school. I wanted to share a meditation of regenerative strength with the group. Folx in TGQ do not attend church, nor do they practice a religion, and yet they are surrounded by divinity school students who frequent the space. Therefore, I was surprised at how a short contemplative exercise actually worked at TGQ.

As an older trans person, the affinity group setting seamlessly situates my identity as a trans pastor administering trans pastoral care. My sense memory allows me to identify individual physical tension by reading peoples' posture. I also draw from my own experiences to complicate the problematic idea of a "gender journey," because I too once identified as nonbinary gender and do not support or amplify the metaphor/definition of gender as a destination. Spirit was collectively felt and present in the space throughout the evening. It was acknowledged when we harnessed our breath and focused inside that action facilitated the grounding for self-love. I led them through a prayer of affirmation without ending it with an "amen" or tying it up in a bow. A reinforced strength was in their eyes as they expressed gratitude for creating a space where they could accept affirmations. I have been struggling with discernment in ministry because I am a nontraditional person in every aspect of the word. Thus, it is in moments and times shared at TGQ that I'm reminded about the rare spaces of worship that exist for trans folx and the role I play in them.

This TGQ felt very body specific not because of the subject matter but because of the physical tension in the room. Trans bodies are demonized, marginalized, and killed by similar social structures of empirical oppression that killed Jesus. We are reminded of how many have been lost every November during Trans Day of Remembrance. Claiming the imago dei in our community is not readily accepted since religion is understood as an oppressive construct by folx ostracized by their families for identifying as LGBTQI. The guidance I offered was not intended to be a prayer, yet it did end up feeling like an affirmation laced with prayer. When I opened my eyes after, I expected to see a bit of cynicism in their eyes because this is not a prayer circle community, but there was only genuine gratitude. A dilemma that was raised for me was the neglect the trans imago dei faces by not having trans-inclusive spaces for the grounding and centering of trans bodies.

By affirming the transgender image of God, societal oppression is no longer legitimized when it claims the trans community and identity are immoral and unethical. Believing that we are all made in the image of God does not have caveats. In *Transgender Warriors*, Leslie Feinberg writes, "We have not always been forced to pass, to go underground, in order to work and live. We have a right to live openly and proudly . . . when our lives are suppressed, everyone is denied an understanding of the rich diversity of sex and gender expression and experience that exist in human society."[1] When the transgender imago dei is denied, the complexity of expressions we all share is denied, and that fosters the cycle of repression and oppression that impacts us all. Similarly, Marcella Althaus Reid's work reminds us not to leave our embodied sexuality, gender expressions, and body at the church door but to bring our whole self to every ritual act. As a queer, trans person, I was able to connect to not being able to leave gender or sexuality at any door, therefore the imago dei is embedded in the theological understanding of all my work.

Compression chest binders make it difficult to breathe deeply since they compress the lungs; people who wear them develop the habit of taking short, shallow breaths. A 10-minute reflection and meditation for a chest-bound group acknowledged our trans enfleshed fullness of being. The trans image of God was reflected in every breath through embodied practice, and the presence of Spirit collapsed the tension to allow for our collective embrace and affirmation of our sacred embodiment.

Chapter Twenty-One

Learning through Our Community

Marcus Hong

Recently, a student sat across from me at the round, honey-colored table in my office and shared with me about the previous semester. At one point, he said, "I didn't realize how difficult it would be emotionally. And spiritually." He had been in ministry at a local nonprofit, working with children. One of the children had suddenly died at the tender age of seven. His voice grew tight as he recalled the memorial service. The room was packed. He was asked to speak. It was the first time he had spoken at a funeral, the first time someone close to him had died. We held silence together. I spent a brief time in his grief. Then we discussed his resources of resilience: talking with friends, asking for grace for assignments, forgoing a January term course to spend time with family. "I'm glad you took time to do those things," I told him. "Me too," he replied.

As you minister with people in a variety of situations, you will sometimes feel like my student felt. Ministry involves *intentionally* engaging with the extremities of our lives: birth, love, grief, joy, death. We must be present to others in those moments. In order to thrive in ministry, we need to learn how to be vulnerable and empathetic in a way that doesn't burn us out. One of the most important resources of resilience is community. In this chapter, we explore what we might expect from learning in community—in particular, its emotional and spiritual impact.

UBUNTU AND MINDSIGHT

You might have noticed that I alternate between the second person (you) and the first person plural (we). When I address you, I implicate myself. You and I are participating in a relationship between writer and reader. As I imagine you, I practice empathy and vulnerability. I consider how you might think differently from me, what you might be experiencing, how you might receive my words. The practice of writing to you enables me to articulate things I did not fully know before I wrote them. Even as I hope my writing moves you, I, too, am changed.

South African theologian Archbishop Desmond Tutu has famously outlined a theology based in the Nguni word *ubuntu*. Recognizing the difficulty of translating this term, Tutu utilizes two key phrases to describe what he means: "my humanity is caught up, is inextricably bound up, in yours" and "a person is a person through other persons."[1] These phrases imbue *ubuntu* with both responsibility and indebtedness. We become who we are through relationships, which should prompt us to consider how we treat others and how others have treated us.[2]

Research in interpersonal neurobiology, spearheaded by Daniel Siegel, echoes this spiritual ideal. Siegel begins by defining "mind" as "an embodied and relational process that regulates the flow of energy and information."[3] With this statement, he indicates that "mind" is neither gray matter in our heads nor some abstract trait untethered from our physical bodies. Rather, our minds—the things we say "change" when we make a decision or are "blown" when surprised by a new insight—are constantly responding (process) to what we experience through every single nerve (embodied) and through our connections with others (relational). You will see these dimensions of mind at work in the way that Trygve D. Johnson and Thomas S. Gatewood III write about biking together or in how Carol Cook and Tyler Mayfield describe setting up their classroom for hospitality and weaving embodiment into their pedagogy.

For Siegel, health involves the "triangle of well-being," three interrelated aspects of the self: mind, relationships, and brain.[4] *Mind* integrates the information and energy received through *relationships* and the embodied sensations that we call the *brain*. Health requires "a balanced and coordinated brain, empathetic and connected relationships, and a coherent and resilient mind."[5] Empathetic relationships "thrive with *integrative communication* in which differences are honored and compassionate connection is cultivated."[6] Understanding that those we engage in ministry are constantly integrating body and relationships helps us to encounter them holistically. It also provides a new perspective on our own resources of resilience. Your care for others is impacted by your mental and physical health and the network of supportive relationships you cultivate. Siegel calls the awareness of this reality in ourselves and others "mindsight."[7]

One example of mindsight is the mindfulness technique that Tara Brach refers to as RAIN. Brach defines mindfulness as being able to "step out of our thoughts about the past and the future" in order to inhabit "a space of presence that is bigger than the particular emotions or thoughts that are going on."[8] In the RAIN technique, we Recognize our feelings, and Allow ourselves to feel them, accepting them as natural responses to our situation. Then, we Investigate why we feel this way. What is my body telling me? What is my inner monologue saying about myself or others? What do I need? Finally, we redirect our emotions through Nurturing, employing resources that provide what we need. This technique neither denies the reality of emotion nor calls on us to stop feeling this way. Rather, it locates the emotion's source and enables us to *regulate* the emotion and find ways to embody fulfillment. As my colleague Justin Reed once noted, it is normal and even right to feel anger at things like injustice. But anger that remains unaddressed often boils over, unintentionally hurting those close to us, particularly if we do not understand the feelings behind it and do not direct it toward the right source.[9]

FOUR TYPES OF COMMUNITY

We become who we are through and with others. We are shaped by unhealthy communities and broken relationships as well as healthy and whole ones. We can also be intentional about who forms us, and about *how* we learn, even from unhealthy communities. In *The Courage to Teach*, Parker Palmer compares four potential focal points for communities: marketing, civics, intimacy, and truth.[10] A market-focused community sees learning as a transaction between provider and consumer. This shines a helpful spotlight on evaluation *by* and accountability *to* those who pay for education. Nevertheless, it relies on what Paolo Freire has called a "banking model" of education, in which the teacher possesses learning that is deposited into the "empty vessels" of students.[11] It also assumes that educational quality depends on students' immediate satisfaction. In this model, learning begins and ends with the classroom transaction. In reality, students bring prior experiences, and learning continues as an ongoing process of reevaluation.

A civics-focused community admits that we may never fully know each other, but we pursue a common goal: "the greatest good for the greatest number."[12] Focusing on a *common* good, instead of personal satisfaction, shifts the learning relationship from teacher and student to a fellowship of learners. Yet, civic norms leave people behind. "In a democratic society, we agree that once the ballots are counted, whoever or whatever receives the highest vote is the leader or the law of the land."[13] The marginalized can be disregarded. This cannot be in a true learning community, which values all voices and attends to those who have been silenced.

The third model, which prioritizes intimacy, addresses our societal disconnection by inviting people to share themselves and be fully known. It relies on trust. This might seem to fit the empathetic community that we have been seeking. In reality, a narrow focus on intimacy can lead to *forced* vulnerability, which is not real vulnerability at all. It can ignore differences in order to push a false commonality. Intimacy, while valuable in learning, cannot be its only goal.

In lieu of these models, Palmer recommends a community of truth gathered around a shared desire to know a personal subject, something greater than themselves. This is not an "object" to be grasped or "conclusions" that are reached and held.[14] Instead, the community lives out "the passionate and disciplined process of inquiry and dialogue itself, as the dynamic conversation of a community that keeps testing old conclusions and coming into new ones."[15] This is an ongoing conversation into which all are invited. Indeed, we can only know truth by hearing every voice. Johnson and Gatewood write about "expanding" their imaginations through this invitation into "something bigger, richer, more complex and true."[16] For Cook and Mayfield, this means "remaining as much as possible in . . . an exploratory posture rather than collapsing into either the certainty of one's Tradition or the self-assurance of one's own life Experience."[17]

In ministry, you will encounter many communities of truth, all reaching for "bigger" things in different ways. For the students who wrote this section's third story, this bigger thing was responding to the divine call to care for others and learning to care for themselves while doing so. Sometimes exploring bigger things will feel more academic, other times more earthy. Sometimes it will be prayerful and playful, other times contentious and uncomfortable. Consider, as you engage these communities, how you are learning. Are you treating learning as simply a transaction? Are you only listening to the dominant voices in the room? Are you forcing others to be intimate or flattening differences in service of a false commonality? Or are you trying to remain open to others, particularly those who have been silenced or ignored; to be challenged, even by those with whom you disagree; and to continue learning for the rest of your life?

EMPATHY AND EXPERIENCE

While intimacy might not be the goal of learning communities, vulnerability and empathy remain important. We cannot consent to be challenged if we cannot be vulnerable. We cannot hear the voices of those silenced or those with whom we disagree if we cannot empathize.

Brené Brown has spent her career studying vulnerability, shame, and empathy. She describes vulnerability as something that "sounds like truth and feels like courage."[18] It means engaging in the "uncertainty, risk, and emotional exposure we face every day."[19] Crucially, vulnerability does not involve revealing everything. It "is based on mutuality and requires boundaries and trust."[20] Verbally flooding others with our experiences creates a barrier to the mutuality that true vulnerability requires and is often a tactic for avoiding empathy.

Brown combines the work of nurse Theresa Wiseman and psychologist Kristin Neff to offer a five-point description of empathy.[21] I have condensed this into four points, since Brown emphasizes that her third and fourth are inextricably interrelated.

1. *Taking other perspectives.* First, we realize that each person sees the world through unique lenses, crafted by experiences and relationships. We cannot remove these lenses nor ignore that our perspectives differ. Instead, we acknowledge our own perspective and then "honor people's perspectives as truth even when they're different from ours."[22] This takes epistemic humility, admitting what we do not know and what we have known wrong. "We cannot practice empathy if we need to be knowers," insists Brown. "If we can't be learners, we cannot be empathetic."[23]
2. *Being nonjudgmental.* This begins with "being aware of where we are the most vulnerable to our own shame."[24] Judgment frequently emerges from our fixation on a perceived lack in ourselves and then evaluates others as doing worse. When we are tempted to judge, we should first consider why we are so bothered by other people's words and actions.
3. *Understanding and communicating another's feelings.* Understanding another person's feelings and communicating that understanding requires "emotional literacy" and being in touch with our feelings.[25] We must both perceive feelings in others and decipher how we are feeling differently *without* transferring our feeling onto them. This involves hearing and believing what other people say they are feeling, which can be challenging because the emotion expressed on our faces is often not the emotion experienced inside. We might express shame as anger, because "our culture is more accepting of anger."[26] Once again, this requires epistemic humility, being willing to have our perception of others' feelings challenged.
4. *Paying attention*, or practicing mindfulness. This means "not over-identifying with or exaggerating our feelings," because "ruminating and getting stuck is as unhelpful as not noticing at all."[27] As we have explored, this is not suppressing or ignoring emotions but recognizing them and directing them toward what is needed.

As we practice vulnerability and empathy, educator and philosopher bell hooks reminds us that we cannot expect anyone to "speak for" their communities of origin in an absolute sense, nor can we use the "authority of experience" to silence others.[28] She compares learning to a recipe. "Imagine," she tells her students, "we are baking bread that needs flour. And we have all the other ingredients but no flour. Suddenly, the flour becomes most important even though it alone will not do."[29]

Experiences alone do not grant authority, but they are valuable when they enable us to understand bigger things together. For hooks, experiences that aim toward bigger things often involve "passion" or "suffering."[30] Therefore, those who have been charged with creating this learning community should recognize the power that they have and utilize it to create space for experiences to be both shared and heard. Still, hooks acknowledges that "there are times when personal experience keeps us from reaching the mountaintop and so we let it go because the weight of it is too heavy."[31] Even more, sometimes all of our knowledge is inadequate, "so we are just there collectively grasping, feeling the limitations of knowledge, longing together, yearning for a way to reach that highest point. Even this yearning is a way to know."[32]

BRAVE SPACE

In a chapter in *The Art of Effective Facilitation*, Brian Arao and Kristi Clemens champion the term "brave space."[33] While affirming the intent of a "safe space," free of "violence of any kind—physical, emotional, and psychological," they conclude that many utilize the term "safe" in order to avoid being transformed by challenging material.[34] "Authentic learning about social justice," they write, and, I would add, truthful and empathetic learning, "often requires the qualities of risk, difficulty and controversy that are defined as incompatible with safety."[35]

Arao and Clemens recommend that brave space learning begin with an agreed-on set of ground rules that they articulate by questioning some of the rules commonly related to safe space. The first rule they address is "agree to disagree." Often, when people "agree to disagree," instead of exploring and understanding how someone else might think differently, they simply state personal opinions without any intent to listen to others, or they "opt out" of conversations that disquiet them.[36] This halts dialogue while exerting privilege. Arao and Clemens advocate instead for "controversy with civility," which leans into the reality that conflict may arise and encourages engaging conflict with respect and care.[37] They contend that "some of the richest learning springs from ongoing explorations of conflict, whereby participants seek to understand an opposing viewpoint."[38] As we have noted, this is a building block of empathy.

The second common ground rule is variously articulated as "don't take things personally," "no judgments," or "it's okay to make mistakes." Arao and Clemens understand the impulse behind this rule: to encourage participants to engage "dispassionately" and therefore enable honesty by reassuring those who might reveal ignorance that they will not be disregarded by their peers.[39] While applauding both honesty and a recognition of imperfection, Arao and Clemens are concerned that the expectation of dispassionate engagement is often rooted in a kind of patriarchal hypermasculinity that values suppressing emotion, ignores the reality that difficult topics provoke emotions, and attempts to "shift responsibility for any emotional impact of what a participant says or shares to the emotionally affected people."[40] Those affected by a harmful statement or action are both hurt and shamed into silence, while the original actor is not called on to change their behavior or learn from their experiences. Arao and Clemens suggest the ground rule "own your intentions and your impact," which puts responsibility for what is said and done back in the hands of each person while acknowledging interrelatedness.

The third common rule is "challenge by choice," which means that "individuals will determine for themselves if and to what degree they will participate in a given activity and this choice will be honored by facilitators and other participants."[41] Arao and Clemens recognize that participation cannot be forced and that some may engage with a challenging activity through internal processing even if they do not actively participate externally. So, while affirming the intent of this ground rule broadly, they also recommend that those facilitating and participating explicitly name the reality of internal processing and ask that everyone "be aware of what factors influence their decisions."[42] This awareness in and of itself may lead to greater reflection and transformation, even for those who choose not to participate in a given activity.

Finally, regarding the fourth and fifth common rules, "respect," and "no attacks," Arao and Clemens recommend discussing what people mean by these words.[43] In a "safe space," most people quickly consent to these rules. But, without concrete examples or details, people may be agreeing without clarity and with definitions that are at odds. Arao and Clemens regularly invite participants to distinguish between a personal attack and a challenge that may lead to discomfort.

Every year, I teach a reflection-based small group course that runs parallel to our required field education experience. For several years, I have begun that course with the following poem, written by movement chaplain and justice doula Micky Scottbey Jones:

> Together we will create brave space.
> Because there is no such thing as a "safe space"—
> We exist in the real world.
> We all carry scars and we have all caused wounds.
> In this space
> We seek to turn down the volume of the outside world,
> We amplify voices that fight to be heard elsewhere,

> We call each other to more truth and love.
> We have the right to start somewhere and continue to grow.
> We have the responsibility to examine what we think we know.
> We will not be perfect.
> This space will not be perfect.
> It will not always be what we wish it to be.
> But It will be *our brave space together,*
> and
> *We will work on it side by side.* [44]

Jones recognizes that, for many, the promise of a "safe space" is a false promise. Many have been harmed by educational systems, ways of learning, and the very texts or experiences that a community might study. For instance, in addressing racism in order to take steps to become antiracist, a community might design a curriculum that honestly confronts and uncovers historical and present practices of racism. For those who have suffered from these practices, this might bring up painful memories, including experiences in which they were not safe. Others who are encountering the truth of these experiences for the first time may feel uncomfortable emotions—guilt, shame, embarrassment, horror. Some are likely to feel personally attacked. For all those participating, this learning requires bravery. It also requires remembering and celebrating the *wholeness* of a person and their history, especially for those who have been oppressed and have been spoken of *only* in the context of their oppression.[45] Finally, it requires honestly admitting, both to ourselves and to others, our current understanding of what we are learning and what we do not yet understand. It calls for the humility to acknowledge what we do not know and to listen deeply when others speak a truth that might transform us, even as it makes us uncomfortable. As Parker Palmer gently advises, "the tension always feels difficult, sometimes destructive. But if I can collaborate with the work it is trying to do rather than resist it, the tension will not break my heart—it will make my heart larger."[46] And, I would add, it will make *our* hearts larger.

QUESTIONS FOR REFLECTION

1. What "bigger things" serve as the subjects around which the learning communities you inhabit are gathered?
2. How have you experienced the transformative "suffering" tension of a learning community that expands your ability to empathize with and love others?
3. What ground rules would you propose as a foundation for the "brave space" of a learning community?

SUGGESTED READING

Brené Brown, *Dare to Lead: Brave Work. Tough Conversations. Whole Hearts.* (New York: Random House, 2018).
bell hooks, *Teaching to Transgress: Education as the Practice of Freedom* (New York: Routledge, 1994).
Parker J. Palmer, *The Courage to Teach: Exploring the Inner Landscape of a Teacher's Life* (San Francisco: Jossey-Bass, 1998).
Daniel J. Siegel, *Mindsight: The New Science of Personal Transformation* (New York: Random House, 2010).

Chapter Twenty-Two

Introducing Theological Education through the Intersection of Bible and Pastoral Care

Carol J. Cook and Tyler D. Mayfield

As theological educators, how intentional are we about the ways in which seminarians commence their education? What part does community formation play, particularly as students embark on their educational journey? These questions guided our discussions during the spring of 2015 as we redesigned a two-week intensive course at our home institution, Louisville Presbyterian Theological Seminary.[1] The course first entered our curriculum in August 2006 and was designed as a vehicle to introduce all entering masters-level students (before the start of the fall semester) to several of our institutional commitments, particularly around antiracism, gender justice, and more recently interfaith cooperation. From the beginning it was ambiguously entitled Transforming Seminary Education, known as TSE. However, over the years, some students had dubbed it "Traumatizing Seminary Education." So, in early conversations about the course redesign, we decided that we wanted to provide students with a gentler but meaningful learning experience that might inspire and encourage them as they moved forward. That hope led us to establish four course goals. In what follows, we share our experience of teaching this "introduction to seminary" class over the course of three summers—2015–2017. After a description of each goal, we include some "evaluative wonderings" that we have continued to ponder as the institution has been in the process of revising its curriculum.

FOUR COURSE GOALS

First, we aspired to set a hospitable, joyful, and inspiring tone at the beginning of students' journey into the wonders of the theologically reflective life. Since students were just getting to know one another, we wanted to begin building community from the outset. Therefore, we created a centerpiece in the middle of a large square of tables that included an abundance of flowers, fruit, and colorful cloths and candles, and we placed small bouquets and name tags at each setting. We had asked students to read Eboo Patel's *Acts of Faith* and write a three-page reflection paper due on the first day of class.[2] Despite fears that the students, who were predominantly Christian, would be put off by beginning their theological education with a frank memoir written by a devout Muslim, students found Patel's emotional and spiritual honesty relatable and disarming. It connected with students' own life and faith journeys in powerful ways and gave them permission to share parts of their own stories more openly with one another.

Although we were not particularly conscious of this while we were team teaching, the easy, respectful rapport that we have with one another and appreciation for each other's discipline went a long way toward fostering an open atmosphere in the classroom. We were surprised that students commented on this and believe it was a gift rather than something manufactured or assumed between all colleagues.

Evaluative wondering: In the end, we believe we did indeed set this type of tone but were left wondering if we were not setting up false expectations for the students since the design of the course is different from most of the courses to come in their seminary education. We did not focus on traditional written assignments and were therefore less able to introduce students to these elements of seminary education. Several students reported finding the transition to philosophical theology, theories, and research papers to be a shock when the fall semester began.

Second, given our respective fields (Carol teaches pastoral theology and Tyler Hebrew Bible), we designed the course at the intersection of pastoral care and Old Testament, inspired by Hopkins and Koppel's *Grounded in the Living Word: The Old Testament and Pastoral Care Practices*. The significance and power of stories shared by both our academic disciplines made that a natural course focus. Each year we found ourselves increasingly emphasizing the importance of listening—to one another, the Bible, and ourselves. We utilized a range of resources, particularly Cari Jackson's *The Gift to Listen: The Courage to Hear* to increase self-awareness about factors that enhance or inhibit effective listening.[3] To assist this process and to build a closer relationship with at least one peer, we assigned a "partners in listening" project.[4] In self-selected pairs, students took turns speaking and listening, then each wrote a self-evaluation of their experience as the listener and then compared those with how the speaker felt heard. Rather than trying to teach "difficult dialogue across differences" more broadly, we found it more manageable to focus specifically on the challenges and rewards of intentional listening as a prerequisite for engaging in authentic conversation, theological education, and all forms of ministry.

Evaluative wonderings: Students found the listening exercises surprisingly challenging and humbling. As is true with most assignments, some students took the assignments more to heart than others, but all tended to reflect substantively about what interfered with their listening and the difference it makes to be "heard into speech."[5]

Third, during our preparation we continued to uncover similarities between the hermeneutical circle of biblical interpretation and the process of theological reflection associated with practical theology, both of which bear resemblance to the experiential learning cycle. Thus, we chose to foreground the process of learning in our respective disciplines over content. Obviously, content matters. But as an introductory tool, we found an overarching schema of the hermeneutical circle to be helpful. To this end, we presented the five interrelated steps Hopkins and Koppel borrowed from Tiffany and Ringe's *Biblical Interpretation: A Roadmap*, which we used as a core textbook.

Hopkins and Koppel summarize the interpretive steps:

1. Beginning the journey at home
2. Encountering the biblical text (This includes paying attention to feelings and reactions that the passage evokes and to the "speed bumps" that slow us down.)
3. Reading the biblical text closely
4. Reading the biblical text contextually
5. Engaging other readers and our communities[6]

Tiffany and Ringe included a final "taking stock of where we are" move, which we labeled a sixth response or action step.[7]

Over the next several days, we introduced the students "step-by-step" to Tiffany and Ringe's roadmap and practiced using the steps in relationship to written texts, paintings, situations, and interpersonal encounters. We continued to draw parallels between how various contexts or "homes" shape all persons in unique ways, including the writers of the Bible and ourselves as readers. We made explicit similarities between Tiffany and Ringe's hermeneutical steps and practical theology's action-reflection method as ways of slowing down reactivity and judgment and making room for discovery and transformation. We continued to practice and then reflect on how we respond to ideas, backgrounds, and theological positions that initially jar us. In doing so, we hoped to help students see connections between different parts of the seminary curriculum, encourage interdisciplinary integration, and experience the generative relationship between theory and practice.

In addition, we engaged the book of Jonah as a class and then in a final small group assignment. The story worked well as a community Bible study because it is short enough that the whole story could be held in mind, and it allowed students to listen to a familiar text with fresh ears. It provided an opportunity for students to realize that they come to the story as an adult with various pre- or misconceptions from childhood and beyond. Jonah also raised questions about reading the Bible as history or metaphor and allowed us to engage diverse commentaries from queer and cross-cultural perspectives.

Evaluative wonderings: Is there any "evidence" for the short- and/or long-term benefit of introducing students to the process of learning and theological reflection at the outset? How could we gauge effectiveness down the road? And while we did not skirt completely the underlying issue of biblical authority, we chose to come at it sideways rather than address it head-on. We acknowledged that that would be something they would continue to work out during the remainder of their time in seminary.

Fourth, consistent with taking a more experiential approach to the course, we wanted to experiment with an embodied, multiple intelligence pedagogy[8] and to intentionally incorporate aspects of intra/interpersonal intelligences in particular. This goal led us to design unconventional assignments, including a final in which small groups of students provided a response to the story of Jonah through their choice of a worship event; a dramatic, artistic, or musical presentation; or a Christian education project for a particular age group. These presentations were incredibly creative, sometimes deeply moving, other times hilarious, and always thought-provoking.

Similarly, we decided not to just read Killen and de Beer's *The Art of Theological Reflection*, which defines it as "the discipline of exploring individual and corporate experience in conversation with the wisdom of a religious heritage."[9] Rather, on the second day of class, when students walked into the classroom, they were met by a giant outline of Killen and de Beer's Venn diagram taped on one of the walls with "Tradition" on one side and "Experience" on the other.[10] We physically walked them through the standpoints of certitude, self-assurance, and exploration[11] by having small groups draw depictions of each of these and in turn paste them in the appropriate sections of the overlapping circles.

With the aid of Brené Brown's immensely popular TED Talk on vulnerability, we discussed the challenges and benefits of remaining as much as possible in Killen and de Beer's exploratory posture while in seminary rather than collapsing into either the certainty of one's tradition or the self-assurance of one's own life experience. Doing this requires making space for emotions as well as the body in theological education. By practicing the cycle, we hoped to increase students' self-awareness and ultimately encourage better management of emotional reactivity.

Evaluative wonderings: Bible courses have an emotional component because they often challenge students' assumptions about the Bible. Combining that with pastoral care's emphasis on self-reflection added to the emotional intensity of the course. Some students were relieved to get back to the Bible; they found talking about Jonah easier than talking about feelings.

CONCLUDING THOUGHTS

There's no getting around that this was an intense classroom experience for all involved. Like the students, we course instructors found it enjoyable, energizing, inspiring, challenging, and exhausting. One of the biggest takeaways for us is that it expanded and solidified our identities as theological educators rather than solely as academics in our respective fields. We learned a great deal from each other's disciplines and teaching styles and believe that we are each better teachers because of this opportunity. It's pretty awesome to be able to participate from the beginning in students' faith, vocational, and communal formation as they appreciate and critique their "embedded theologies" and psychologies and start to construct more deliberative and life-giving approaches.[12]

QUESTIONS FOR REFLECTION

1. Carol Cook and Tyler Mayfield name the reality that theological education can be as much of an emotional journey as an intellectual one. What emotions have you felt while undertaking theological education?
2. The redesign of the Transforming Seminary Education course emerged with four goals, all aimed at fostering community, briefly summarized as fostering hospitality and joy, encouraging intentional listening, foregrounding the process of learning, and experimenting with an embodied, multiple intelligence pedagogy. When have you experienced being welcomed, heard, challenged, and holistically engaged?
3. Cook and Mayfield demonstrate their own ability to remain in an exploratory posture by ending each goal with a set of evaluative wonderings. What questions or tensions continue to haunt you or leave you wondering?

Chapter Twenty-Three

Providential Friendship

Trygve D. Johnson and Tee S. Gatewood III

> A friend is a second self.
> —Aristotle

"Providence" is a fancy word the church uses to suggest that God is real, and this real God shows up, in real time, and real places, in order to offer people his spiritual power, guidance, and care. Of all the doctrines of the church, Providence may be one of the most captivating and mysterious. Its discernment requires a contemplative nature, asking one to reflect on the practical ways God shows up to shape and sustain our lives. It's easy to get wrong, as self-deception is one of the easiest temptations in the Christian life.

Providence is a doctrine that, at least in my life, makes sense looking backward. When I review my life, where I see Providence the most noticeably are in the defining friendships. That is to say, when I look backward, it is through the friends God has put in my life that I see how God brought into my life a surprising blessing. For this reason, I see and value my friendships as a particular gift, or grace, even a form of wealth, from a living God who cared to show up in my real life. Not every friendship merits this divine recognition. Only in those rare friendships can I trace divine fingerprints on my own story that would cause me to say this is a "providential friendship."

My criterion for discerning whether a friendship is providential requires two fundamental qualities. The first characteristic is that a "providential friendship" involves a sense of being known and valued. The gift of being understood—of being truly seen by another—is a rare experience. I have had this intimate gift with few people, but each time it has happened, it has birthed a lasting and meaningful friendship. The second facet of a providential friend includes the first but also brings with it the sense that this relationship is about something larger—something consequential—a feeling that the relationship may exist to serve a purpose that transcends the relationship itself.

Maybe one way to describe this quality is that the friendship brings with it a kind of shared imagination—a sense that each offers a tacit trust of the other—as both are working, in their own ways, toward the same goal, which inspires a work that is worthy of one's life. When these two aspects come together—the sense of being known and a shared imagination of purpose—I can look back and notice the hints and guesses of God's presence in my life. I can see Providence.

When looking back over my life, there has been no better providential friend, or gift of grace, or currency of wealth, than I have had with my friend Tee Gatewood. Tee has been that friend who has "seen" me and not looked away. He now qualifies as an old friend because we have traveled together through our early to middle age of life. He knows my particular faults and yet never looks for fault. He sees my gifts and never feels the need to compete. In his presence, I discover the rare experience of being in communion.

Together our communion shares a mutual respect and admiration for the other but also shares a common vision for our vocation—a particular commitment to the pastoral life that transcends our relationship. That bond—rooted in a common vision—inspires our pastoral imagination to recommit ourselves to the work, the sacrifice, the calling of Word and Sacrament each week. This, though, requires the recognition that our friendship needs attention to intentionality if our gift is to be experienced as a sustaining grace.

SUSTAINING THE PROVIDENTIAL GIFT

"Call Trygve Johnson, Private." I only have one phone number labeled 'private' in all my contacts. It is the number I call that rings directly in Tryg's office. It is the number I call when I need to get to my friend without the possibility of interference.

Dialing that number for over a decade, I have learned a fundamental truth—namely, the providential gift of friendship is sustained by conversation. A vast amount of my friendship with Tryg has been sustained by conversation on the phone; Tryg in Holland, Michigan, getting a call from Tee in Banner Elk, North Carolina, or Trygve on the move in the great white North calling Tee in the Deep South.

In these conversations on the phone, we continue to see each other even though we aren't literally seeing each other. That is the case because we can share the struggles of being committed to our calling. We can share the complexity of leading and blessing those who work with us and those we work for. We can be honest about the sacrifice of time and pride, being right, and getting what we feel we deserve. And through it all we can converse about the holy conversation. We can talk on the phone about the conversation that we are having with the triune God through the constant reading and eating of Scripture.

What are you hearing? What are you sharing? And how? How are you trying to speak to your people in this time and place, in the midst of this crisis or that conflict? How are you bringing all of who you are to God to listen so that with all of who you are you can then turn and speak the truth in love? How are you participating in what the Spirit is doing in Christ? These are some of our questions.

It hasn't always been this way. Some of our best conversations have taken place on rough roads through dark valleys and over great mountain peaks, literally. Tryg and I are cyclists. We are friends that ride together. One of the great things about riding the earth together is that it gives you time and space to talk while you are focused on a common destination. C. S. Lewis often talked about friendship as a side-by-side reality. He loved to walk and talk and smoke with Ronald and Charles. Tryg and I don't walk often, but we have clipped in and ridden together, first in Scotland and then on the Blue Ridge Parkway.

The Blue Ridge Parkway is 470 miles long. It is one of the great American roads. The northern terminus is in Rockfish, Virginia. The southern terminus is in Cherokee, North Carolina. In between are innumerable climbs, memorable descents, expansive vistas, dense forest, racoons and turkeys, tunnels and trees, and lots of space for conversation. Sometimes we talk with our mouths, while at other times we talk with our legs. Sometimes we talk to each other, and other times we simply end up talking to ourselves. In the rain and cold and heat we have ridden together. Mile after mile we have talked together and seen something in each other that couldn't have been seen in other conditions or in any other way, side by side, in pain and glory, with the wind at our backs and in our faces.

Though enthusiasts, what we discovered on our bikes is that these rides are an apt metaphor for our sustained friendship. Our lives, like the Blue Ridge, have remarkable vistas, some long and painful climbs, and dramatic descents. On these climbs we each have to ride at our own pace. We have to stay within ourselves, as our abilities are able. Living and riding in the backyard of the mountains of North Carolina, Tee is a stronger, lighter cyclist. Tee can ride up the long ascending grades with the smoothness and ease of a mountain goat, whereas Tryg has a Nordic shape and is built to suffer, with strong will and an athletic heart. We learn on the bike that our conversation is sustained at a different pace. We learn not to compete or compare ourselves to each other on the bike. We learn how to encourage, and how to challenge, and how to empathize. Riding together teaches us how to stay within ourselves, each doing what we can, at our own pace. We have to dig deep, and explore the layers within, in order to be able to discover what is really buried deep in the soul. But even though we go different speeds, our end is the same. Sooner or later, we both get there, and when we do we share a common meal and process the thoughts that are unearthed during the daily revolutions.

As we process what we learn on the bike, it's interesting how it is also reflective of our ministries. We have to pastor out of who we are, within the confines of our limits, not in a hurry but moving toward a common end. In this, our friendship is sustained by the awareness of the narrow road we need to travel together, to encourage each other, challenge each other, a road where we discover, though with difficulty, that Christ is not only the way, he is also the destination.

THE CONVERSATION

Ultimately, Tryg and I are having a conversation about Jesus, about all the ways that he is the way to the Father, into the world, into relationship with others, into a life with others in the church as pastors and preachers. Over the years and over the phone and over the miles, we are having this conversation about life and learning together. In this conversation there is by the gift of the Spirit a true knowing and being known, learning and teaching, blessing and calling out to find the narrow gate and the hard road. Things come to life in this conversation and sometimes come back to life. Sometimes there is also crucifixion and confession, the sharing of the things we have gotten accustomed to hiding and might prefer to avoid.

In his little book *How to Think*, Alan Jacobs asserts that no one learns to think for themselves or by themselves. "Thinking is," according to Jacobs, "necessarily, thoroughly, and wonderfully social. Everything you think is a response to what someone else thought and said." Thinking is wonderfully social. The society of our particular conversation is also wonderfully wide. That is because Tryg and I live and move and have our ecclesial lives in different places with different kinds of people. We also like different kinds of books and music. There is sufficient overlap for appreciation and sufficient difference for new voices to enter in and expand the conversation. The particular gift of that is that our imaginations are consistently being invited into something bigger, richer, more complex and true.

In a moment when pastors are under constant pressure to reduce their callings to be "shop-keepers" for the spiritual consumer, there is a deep need for conversational partners who can expand our pastoral imaginations in this dynamic way. The pastoral imagination is one that is rooted not only in the Scripture but also in the community, and more precisely in friendship. This imagination, nurtured and tended by intentional friendship, is needed if pastors are going to be faithful to their primary callings to serve the church as servants of Word and Sacrament.

Tee and I feel the seductive voices and the temptations that lead away from the calling of a pastoral theologian, who cares for the souls of one's people and the Gospel witness of the church. We have found little incentive from our congregations, or institutions, to help pastors read and study and few resources from our instructional schools to encourage needed networks for like-minded pastors to share together substantive and sustained study and conversation in the context of spiritual friendship. What we have learned, through years of talking together, is that our callings require the structured and intentional work of friendship. It does not just happen. A providential friendship needs the work of an intentional conversation.

But that pastoral relationship requires sustained friendship—dare I say, providential friends—who commit to talk, eat and drink, to process our marriages and parenting, to bare each other's souls and to share each other's burdens in the process. Tee has been, is, that friend to me, and I have been that friend to him. Our communion happens in the rare times we are together but most often on the phone, or in the rare times we get together in person, on a bike, and in a virtual reading group that we christened The Kingfisher Society.

THE KINGFISHER SOCIETY

One of the patron saints of our shared friendship and vocation is Eugene Peterson. Peterson believed the pastoral life must be lived and experienced in the context of relationships. If one's theology could not be lived in a relationship, then it was not a theology fit for the Gospel of a God who becomes incarnate. Peterson's pastoral writings offer working pastors the gift of a conversation partner who takes them and their vocation and calling seriously. His writings show how pastors can become more biblically rooted, theologically thick, missionally aspiring, while offering others, and themselves, an expansive emotional canopy that gives shade to our shared human experience in Christ. When reading Peterson, I get the sense that I am invited to explore the large geography of God's world. He has inspired me, and a generation of pastors, to believe that there has never been a better time to be a pastor.

Our friendship, and our vocation, requires a regular give and take, a sharing of our learning, and the practice of a common vocabulary in regular conversation. This conversation is our learning community. This is why we started The Kingfisher Society.

The kingfisher was a favorite metaphor of Eugene Peterson, who served as both a mentor and model for the pastoral life that Tee and I are pursuing. The kingfisher is a bird who will dive down into the water 30, 40, 50 times before getting a fish. Peterson loved this thought—because this was the "king" of getting fish. Would we keep trying at our work—our sermon—30, 40, 50 times to get it right? We set up a weekly schedule of reading a Peterson book a month, memorizing a psalm a week, and conversation.

This rhythm of reading together and praying together and talking on the phone and on the bike has a strange focus: to catch people. Jesus, in Matthew 4, calls the disciples to follow him. He calls them with the strange promise that they will fish for or catch men and women, children and enemies. One of the blessings of the way Jesus called people into this ministry then and now is that he did not call them as individuals but as persons in a relationship. First Simon, who would be called Peter, is called with Andrew. Then James and John, the sons of Zebedee. Jesus calls them and calls them together and ultimately calls them friends. When we start to become what we are in Christ, there is a strange joy and great blessing: the joy of discovering that we are not alone and that we are blessed together to turn out and bless others together.

Some days when I turn onto Hickory Nut Gap and start the windy climb to Arbor Dale Presbyterian Church, I see a kingfisher. This kingfisher often "catches fire" from the powerline over the Elk River. He sits and then swoops. He waits and watches and then dives. I know that if I see him and listen, I can hear him crying, "What I do is me: for that I came."[1] When I see that kingfisher, I think of Tryg and our friendship. I consider the way that we are diving and waiting, watching and diving, over and over. In those moments I remember that I am not alone. I am not driving up this road to serve at this church by myself; I have a friend. I have a friend who reminds me of who I am and who I am in Christ for others.

In friendship we have experienced a community of learning that not only teaches us about ourselves; we have found a new life with the triune God—this God who is for us and who through a providential friendship is with us for the work he has called us to pursue in faithful obedience in the same direction.

QUESTIONS FOR REFLECTION

1. Johnson and Gatewood write about providential friendships in which one feels "truly seen" and drawn to a purpose that transcends the relationship itself. Have you ever experienced a "providential" relationship?
2. Communities and relationships are often built around shared activities, like biking and being pastoral leaders for Johnson and Gatewood. Around what kinds of activities do you desire to build meaningful, lasting relationships?

3. What do you think is essential to maintaining the kinds of relationships in which we are truly seen, heard, and understood?

Chapter Twenty-Four

Nourishment for the Long Journey of Ministry

Abigale Embry, Val Goins, Lindsay Ross-Hunt, and Sandra Monroe

NOTE: *This memoir/case story was created communally by four recent graduates of Louisville Presbyterian Theological Seminary, all of whom took part in a small-group, reflection-based course known as Practical Theology in Congregations (PTC). This course took place alongside a required nine-month congregational field education placement. Their group included eight students. The memoir/case story was written by weaving together memories shared by the authors.*

ABIGALE: We used our class time to share case studies, design projects, and learn theory and practices behind working in congregations. What I enjoyed the most was the diversity within the class in both placements and the past congregational experience my peers brought with them. Because each of our settings were quite different, I was exposed not only to my own placement but to several other placements as well in hearing my peers share during case studies and check-in time. Concerns or celebrations from each student added to my knowledge of what is possible in congregational work, knowledge that could have taken years to gain on my own.

SANDRA: We were a small, intimate group, and our work in this environment was not to outdo each other in academic superiority but to share each of our experiences so that we could all learn from the successes and the failures within the group. I think it helped that we also met in the evenings, when we were nearly the only people on campus, making our experience even more intimate. We further enhanced the intimate nature of the group by agreeing as a community to eat and share meals together weekly before class with a voluntary potluck. It collectively eased that pressure of trying to decide every week if we could fit in dinner before class or if we needed to miss it. We knew it would be there, and if it was our week to bring something, we could "bite the bullet" and provide, because we knew we only had to do that a couple of times the whole semester. There is something to be said for feeding each other—knowing we were relying on each other once a week for basic biological needs. We also shared personal joys and sorrows around this table of feasting and learning—sometimes sharing things that we didn't want to have shared outside of the group. This further developed and was proof of our trust in each other and our ability to be vulnerable.

LINDSAY: I had missed the first meeting of the class due to the fact that my father had died just before the start of term. When I finally walked in the second night, I realized it was quite a small group, so "checking out" or "phoning it in" weren't going to be options for me. At the same time, I was relieved to discover that this community was one in which I could participate without having to check that reality at the door—that I did not have to pretend that everything was fine or great but that I could hold that part of my story with tenderness, even as I was invited to hold others' stories with tenderness too.

VAL: Learning in community mirrored the worlds we eventually inhabited as pastors, pastoral counselors, and chaplains. Communities foster deep relationships in which a wide range of emotions can be shared. While seminary prepared us for the mechanics of ministry, community prepared us for the *lives* we will live in ministry.

LINDSAY: The course was structured in such a way that we engaged in various spiritual practices for a period of time throughout the year—"trying them on," so to speak, so as to see what might resonate and sustain. Early on, we engaged in *lectio divina*, a practice of contemplative and meditative Scripture reading. At the time, my own grief still felt very close and nearly ever-present.

In the classroom one night we were invited to become still—something that felt exceedingly elusive to me in the anxiety of my grief—and prepare for the reading. Our professor began to read from 1 Kings the story of the prophet Elijah fleeing to the wilderness, hiding under a tree in weariness and hopelessness. Though those were feelings with which I could surely resonate, it was not until I heard the angel's words, "Get up and eat, otherwise the journey will be too much for you," that I heard the text speaking to me that day. Something in those words caught my attention. The inescapable numbness I felt when I had first sat down began, ever so slowly, to crack open and dissipate.

Beginning with spiritual practice together in this way created the container that our whole selves were not only welcome in this space but expected and even needed. We would, after all (hopefully!), be engaged in ministry as whole persons at some point or another, and in fact, many of us already were. To assume that we could somehow disconnect our emotions and experiences from our learning and our practice would be just as much a fallacy in the classroom as it would be in "the real world." The invitation in our times together over the course of the year was always how to understand and engage those experiences in a way that was constructive for our practice of ministry—to use the time and space together to explore together in community what that might look like.

Those words from 1 Kings also became a kind of mission statement for this community for me, both in terms of the actual food we shared as we gathered together each week and in the posture with which I wanted to approach our time together: here was an opportunity to learn from and support each other as we explored our various ministerial contexts.

ABIGALE: I enjoyed that it gave us a certain amount of accountability with one another to keep persisting when things felt overwhelming. It also had an added layer of accountability with the site supervisors as well. One of my peers shared that she was feeling weighed down with the amount of administrative work she was doing, such as designing and printing bulletins each week. When she shared this with me, I was able to encourage her to seek more experiences in her role that would fit her personal and professional goals. She might not have known it wasn't typical for an intern to do an unusually large amount of administrative work if she had not been able to share that with the class. It was important to share these experiences so that we could make sure we were using our time wisely during that year for our own growth in a way that balanced well with our placement's needs.

LINDSAY: Our PTC cohort was precisely the thing I needed and the thing I wished I'd had from day one in seminary. The overarching goal of our time together was not just "how to practice ministry" but how to practice ministry as whole persons. As ministers, we cannot neglect ourselves and hope to assist others with any sort of sustainability. It was in the space created between those colleagues—over shared hodgepodge meals, laughter, tears, and exasperation—that learning felt integrative. Feelings were welcome in the class, and the process of sharing and processing them within the group helped direct them toward constructive ends.

SANDRA: This small group enabled me to learn an important life lesson through a hymnbook. During that year my congregational placement was with a very small (12–16 people attending weekly Sunday worship) southern Indiana Presbyterian congregation. The meeting place was literally in the middle of a cornfield, and many of the congregants were from the same family of origin.

While planning my first worship service, I had picked several hymns from the "red hymnbook" they had been using since the 1960s. I had trouble finding enough hymns to fit my theology and supplement the message I had prepared, but after an exhaustive search I settled on four, which was the number of hymns they normally had in a worship service. I submitted my bulletin outline to the congregation member who assembled and printed the bulletin for every service. When I arrived at the meeting place for the first service I would lead with them, I noticed all the hymns had been changed. None of them supported my message or were linked to the verses I had chosen. The person constructing the bulletin arrived before anyone else and said, "I had to change the hymns you had. We didn't know any of those."

This was the beginning of a long struggle for me with this community and their hymns. I tried to choose one hymn and let the bulletin constructor select the other three. I once communicated with the pianist ahead of time regarding a selection that wasn't in the hymnal but appeared to me to be a simple two-line hymn that could be easily repeated. My daughter happened to visit that week, so there were two of us singing it. No one else.

I just couldn't understand why these Presbyterians wanted to sing about the "blood of Jesus" and "the Lord" every week. The words to these hymns rubbed against my theology, concepts and commitments I had learned through planning worship services on the seminary campus and in my communications and gender course during the pursuit of my bachelor's degree.

My frustrations continued through the first three months. Then, one Sunday during fellowship, the person who put the bulletins together said, "I love that hymn we sang today. Every time we sing that I can hear my daddy right beside me." Her father had been deceased for 30 years. That was the beginning of my realization that these hymns held their history as a congregation. These hymnals from 50 years ago held the voices of their ancestors. These hymns, through singing, held their faith. The words and their individual meanings and the theology they wove were not of consequence to the people in the congregation. It was the memories associated with them that mattered. When I came in and tried to change the hymns, it felt like I was trying to change their history and rip their ancestors away from them.

An exclamation point was added when we had a hymn sing and invited the church from "town" to come out to the country and join us. The entire service was the congregation singing hymns they picked out of the "red hymnal." The only stipulation was that they had to explain why that hymn was important to them. The members of the other congregation were absolutely delighted to be running their fingers through all of these old hymns. Many of them shared memories associated with the hymns and even shed a few tears in the telling and the singing.

Now that I had come to understand their intimate connection to this music, I needed to come to terms with my aversion to it. This was only possible through sharing in the group. As the "saga of the hymnbooks" continued through that first semester, it became a "what happened this week" story, like an ongoing news update for my peers. Then someone in the group asked me, "What do those hymns remind you of?" That was it. The tears began to flow, and I began to share that those words about an "almighty Lord" and "the blood of Jesus" reminded me of the Jesus my parents had been taught about as children. It was a version of Jesus my parents had learned to distance themselves from in their adulthood. In these hymns were the images of God my parents had ridiculed throughout my childhood. Without that one question and without my trust in sharing my truth with the group, I couldn't have figured that out. I would have stood in my righteous academic beliefs and would have missed the human connection.

Once I came to terms with what those hymns had symbolized for me and where my deep emotions were coming from, as well as those of the congregation, I was able to let go. As things ended that year with the congregation, I was able to bring a new hymn to them from the twenty-first-century revised Presbyterian hymnal, and they were able to sing with me. On that day I sang with tears in my eyes.

VAL: Midway through the year, one of the students in our seminary cohort died. While she was being treated for leukemia, we knew how sick she was, but her death came unexpectedly and caught many of us unprepared. We were grieving individually while living in the pressurized world of academia, where we were unable to mourn her loss and seek closure.

The PTC community was able to openly talk about our loss. We shared anger and frustration. We lamented together and spoke openly of the guilt and numbness that we felt. Our hearts were able to heal through the shared experience of mourning.

As candidates for ministry and students, we knew the correct prayers to pray, the liturgies to follow. However, for some of us, we had not before experienced such a close loss of someone our own age. We may have even performed funerals in our parish, but many had never processed the grief of a close, personal loss. Sharing and commemorating our fellow student in the safety of the PTC classroom has helped me not only heal from that loss but also empathize with my parishioners during their loss. I learned firsthand the value of communal mourning and grief sharing. I have used the time spent with my classmates as inspiration for joining the families in their grief journey at funerals I have performed.

The techniques of ministry can be taught in a lecture, the mechanics of ministry can be written about in a book, but the sharing of lives necessary to practical theology can only be learned in community.

QUESTIONS FOR REFLECTION

1. Lindsay Ross-Hunt mentions a practice of *lectio divina* that enabled her to move through her grief into the community. What spiritual practices enable you to constructively encounter your emotions in order to be present with others?
2. Have you ever experienced situations like Sandra Monroe's, in which something that seemed like a hurdle to ministry ended up revealing more about who you are as a person and as a minister?
3. What knowledge have you gained that you have only truly been able to learn in community?

Notes

INTRODUCTION

1. Donald Schon, *The Reflective Practitioner: How Professionals Think in Action* (New York: Basic Books, 1983), 54.
2. Quoted in Cat Williams, *Stay Calm and Content: No Matter What Life Throws at You* (Bloomington, IN: Author House, 2012), 122.

1. LEARNING THROUGH OUR EXPERIENCE

1. Eduard Lindeman, *The Meaning of Adult Education* (Montreal: Harvest House, 1961), 6.
2. Malcolm Gladwell, *Blink: The Power of Thinking without Thinking* (New York: Back Bay Books, 2007).
3. Pastoral imagination, a special kind of intelligence nurtured by the process of learning through experience, is described well by Craig Dykstra, "Pastoral and Ecclesial Imagination," in *For Life Abundant* (Grand Rapids, MI: Eerdmans, 2008), 41–61. The process of pastoral imagination's formation is delineated in *Learning Pastoral Imagination: A Five-Year Report on How New Ministers Learn in Practice*, by Christian A. B. Scharen and Eileen R. Campbell-Reed, https://auburnseminary.org/wp-content/uploads/2016/02/Learning-Pastoral-Imagination.pdf.
4. I'm appreciative of Grace Ji-Sun Kim's and Susan Shaw's helpful *Intersectional Theology: An Introductory Guide* (Minneapolis: Fortress Press, 2018).
5. See chapter 3.
6. Flora Keshgegian, *Time for Hope: Practices for Living in Today's World* (New York: Continuum, 2006), 100.
7. Robert Coles, *Children of Crisis* (Boston: Little, Brown, 2003), xv–xvi.
8. Howard W. Stone and James O. Duke address the concepts of embedded and deliberative theology in *How to Think Theologically*, 3rd edition (Minneapolis: Fortress, 2013).
9. O. L. M. Fayanju, "Hiding in Plain Sight," *JAMA* 322, no. 22 (2019): 2173–74.
10. S. Joseph Levine, *Getting to the Core: Reflections on Teaching and Learning* (Okemos, MI: Learner Associates.net, 2005), 101–2.
11. Thank you to Ashlee Floding for creating figures 1 and 2.

12. Each synthesizes work done before them, including foremostly educators and theorists: William James, Eduard Lindeman, John Dewey, Jean Piaget, Carl Rogers, Kurt Lewin, Lev Vygotsky, Paulo Freire, and Mary Parker Follett.

13. David A. Kolb, *Experiential Learning: Experience as the Source of Learning and Development*, 2nd ed. (Upper Saddle River, NJ: Pearson Education, 2015), see especially chapter 2, "The Process of Experiential Learning."

14. Jason Byassee, "Engaging in Preaching," in *Engage: A Theological Field Education Toolkit*, ed. Matthew Floding (New York: Rowman & Littlefield, 2017), 53.

15. David Fleming, SJ, *What Is Ignatian Spirituality?* (Chicago: Loyola Press, 2008), https://www.ignatianspirituality.com/ignatian-prayer/the-spiritual-exercises/pray-with-your-imagination/.

16. See chapter 7.

17. Names of students, except chapter contributors, have been changed to preserve confidentiality, and each has given permission to use their story. "Engaging in Theological Reflection," in *Engage: A Theological Field Education Toolkit*, ed. Matthew Floding (Lanham, MD: Rowman & Littlefield, 2017), 38.

18. Étienne Wenger, *Communities of Practice* (New York: Cambridge University Press, 1998), 3.

19. Étienne Wenger, *Introduction to Communities of Practice*, https://wenger-trayner.com/introduction-to-communities-of-practice/.

20. Wenger, *Communities of Practice*, 90.

21. The definitions of these concepts are sourced in Lave and Wenger, *Situated Learning*; Wenger, *Communities of Practice*; Wenger, McDermott, and Snyder, *Cultivating Communities of Practice*; and further information kindly shared by Étienne Wenger through personal communication.

22. Wenger, *Communities of Practice*, 227.

23. Jean Lave and Étienne Wenger, *Situated Learning: Legitimate Peripheral Participation* (New York: Cambridge University Press, 1991), 3.

24. Tradition/tradition, capital *T* Tradition meaning the church catholic, small *t* meaning the tradition that we personally inhabit within the Tradition (e.g., Lutheran).

2. A TEACHING TRAVELOGUE

1. Frances A. Maher and Mary Kay Thompson, *The Feminist Classroom: Dynamics of Gender, Race, and Privilege* (New York: Basic Books, 1994), 9–10.

2. Origen, Fragmenta ex commentariis in epistulam Ii ad Corinthios.

5. LEARNING THROUGH OUR STORIES

1. Donald E. Polkinghorne, *Narrative Knowing* (Albany: State University of New York Press, 1988), 30.

2. Janice McDrury and Maxine Alterio, *Learning through Storytelling in Higher Education: Using Reflection and Experience to Improve Learning* (London: Routledge, 2016), 44. Quoting Chaille and Britain (1991), 11.

3. Jack Mezirow, "Learning to Think Like an Adult: Core Concepts of Transformation Theory," in *Learning as Transformation: Critical Perspectives on a Theory in Progress*, ed. Jack Mezirow and Associates (San Francisco: Jossey-Bass, 2000), 26.

4. Laura S. Foote, "Re-storying Life as a Means of Critical Reflection: The Power of Narrative Learning," *Christian Higher Education* 14, no. 3 (2015): 123. Quoting Merriam et al., 2007.

5. Mary Field Belenky and Ann V. Stanton, "Inequality, Development, and Connected Knowing," in *Learning as Transformation*, ed. Jack Mezirow and Associates (San Francisco: Jossey-Bass, 2000), 73.
6. Mezirow, "Learning to Think Like an Adult," 3.
7. Polkinghorne, *Narrative Knowing*, 18.
8. M. Carolyn Clark and Marsha Rossiter, "'Now the Pieces Are in Place . . .': Learning through Personal Storytelling in the Adult Classroom," *New Horizons in Adult Education & Human Resource Development* 20, no. 3 (2006): 19.
9. Polkinghorne, *Narrative Knowing*, 112.
10. Sharan B. Merriam, Rosemary S. Caffarella, and Lisa M. Baumgartner, eds., *Learning in Adulthood: A Comprehensive Guide* (San Francisco: Jossey-Bass, 2000), 214.
11. Foote, "Re-storying Life as a Means of Critical Reflection," 122.
12. Polkinghorne, *Narrative Knowing*, 18.
13. Ibid., 106.
14. Clark and Rossiter, "'Now the Pieces Are in Place . . . ,'" 16.
15. Mezirow, "Learning to Think Like an Adult," 20.
16. M. H. Z. Kish, *Using Vignettes to Develop Higher Order Thinking and Academic Achievement in Adult Learners in an Online Environment* (Dissertation, 2004).
17. McDrury and Alterio, *Learning through Storytelling in Higher Education*, 31.
18. Clark and Rossiter, "'Now the Pieces Are in Place . . . ,'" 4.
19. Rossiter and Clark, in Merriam et al., *Learning in Adulthood*, 210.
20. Patricia Cranton, "Individual Differences and Transformative Learning," in *Learning as Transformation*, ed. Jack Mezirow and Associates (San Francisco: Jossey-Bass, 2000), 195.

9. LEARNING THROUGH UNLEARNING

1. Alvin Toffler, *Future Shock* (New York: Random House, 1970), 414.
2. The full text of Toffler's Gerjuoy quote is as follows: "The *new* education must teach the individual how to classify and reclassify information, how to evaluate its veracity, how to change categories when necessary, how to move from the concrete to the abstract and back, *how to look at problems from a new direction—how to teach himself.* Tomorrow's illiterate will not be the man who can't read; he will be the man who has not learned how to learn" (my emphasis).
3. By the learning cycle, I am talking not about how people learn from their experiences (e.g., David Kolb's four-stage cycle of experiential learning) but about how people's learning advances through *unlearning their previous experiences and prior knowledge*. And notably the learning cycle keeps turning.
4. Toffler, *Future Shock*, 414.
5. Mark Twain, "Taming the Bicycle," http://storyoftheweek.loa.org/2017/11/taming-bicycle.html. Written around 1886 and first published in 1917. For the quoted words, see Louis J. Budd, ed., *Mark Twain: Collected Tales, Sketches, Speeches, & Essays 1852–1890* (New York: The Library of America, 1992), 893.
6. "The Backwards Brain Bicycle—Smarter Every Day 133," posted on April 25, 2015, https://www.youtube.com/watch?v=MFzDaBzBlL0. (My emphasis.)
7. I am here leaving out the change of the emotional and volitional aspect of our mindset, even though I recognize the fact that "changing people's minds requires empathetic exploration of their attachment to prior viewpoints." L. O. Aranye Fradenburg and Eileen A. Joy, "Unlearning: A Duologue," in *The Pedagogics of Unlearning*, ed. Aidan Seery and Éamonn Dune (Goleta, CA: Punctum Books, 2016), 167.
8. Courtney E. Ackerman, "What Is Neuroplasticity? A Psychologist Explains," https://positivepsychology.com/neuroplasticity/.
9. John D. Caputo, "Teaching the Event: Deconstruction, Hauntology, and the Scene of Pedagogy," in *The Pedagogics of Unlearning*, ed. Aidan Seery and Éamonn Dune (Goleta, CA: Punctum Books, 2016), 125.

10. Ian Hacking, "Introductory Essay," in Thomas S. Kuhn, *The Structure of Scientific Revolutions: 50th Anniversary Edition*, 4th ed. (Chicago: University of Chicago Press, 2012), xxvi (my emphasis). The first edition was published in 1962, the second in 1970, and the third in 1996.

11. For instance, Hans Küng and David Tracy applied Kuhn's concept of *paradigm change* to theology, David Bosch to missiology, and a journal called *Educational Technology* to education. See Hans Küng and David Tracy, eds., *Paradigm Change in Theology: A Symposium for the Future* (New York: Crossroad, 1989). David J. Bosch, *Transforming Mission: Paradigm Shifts in Theology of Mission* (Maryknoll, NY: Orbis, 1991). "Paradigm Change in Education," *Educational Technology* 54, no. 3 (May–June 2014).

12. Jack Mezirow, *Education for Perspective Transformation: Women Re-entry Programs in Community College* (New York: Center for Adult Education, Teachers College, Columbia University, 1978). This study was inspired by the transformative learning experience of his wife, Edee Mezirow, who had returned to college as an adult to complete her undergraduate degree.

13. Jack Mezirow, "Transformative Learning Theory," in *Transformative Learning in Practice: Insights from Community, Workplace, and Higher Education*, ed. Jack Mezirow, Edward W. Taylor, and Associates (San Francisco: Jossey-Bass, 2009), 22 (original emphasis).

14. Jack Mezirow, "How Critical Reflection Triggers Transformative Learning," in *Fostering Critical Reflection in Adulthood: A Guide to Transformative and Emancipatory Learning*, ed. Jack Mezirow and Associates (San Francisco: Jossey-Bass, 1990), 1–20.

15. The positive effect of critical reflection on unlearning as well as that of unlearning on transformation has been confirmed even by quantitative research done by Makoto Matsuo, a professor in the Graduate School of Economics and Business Administration at Hokkaido University. See "Why Unlearning Matters? How to Unlearn?," https://www.socialsciencespace.com/2020/01/why-unlearning-matters-how-to-unlearn/.

16. Mezirow was deeply influenced by, among others, John Dewey's progressive education theory, of which the goal is to educate students to become independent thinkers and lifelong learners; by Paulo Freire's critical pedagogy, of which the goal is emancipation from oppression through an awakening of the critical consciousness; by Jürgen Habermas's theory of communicative learning, of which the goal is a mutual agreement through critical reflection and critical self-reflection; and by Roger Gould's theory of transformation, of which the goal is to *give up* various *illusions* and myths held over from childhood.

17. Regarding the 10 "phases of meaning becoming clarified" that our transformation generally follows, see Jack Mezirow, "Learning to Think Like an Adult: Core Concepts of Transformation Theory," in *Learning as Transformation: Critical Perspectives on a Theory in Progress*, ed. Jack Mezirow and Associates (San Francisco: Jossey-Bass, 2000), 22.

18. John Willinsky, *Learning to Divide the World: Education at Empire's End* (Minneapolis: University of Minnesota Press, 1998), 262.

19. "John Suler's Zen Stories to Tell Your Neighbors," http://truecenterpublishing.com/zenstory/emptycup.html.

20. "Christianity is so self-righteous that I do not see the future for it. It wants to teach. It does not want to learn." Kosuke Koyama, "Christianity Suffers from 'Teacher Complex,'" in *Mission Trends No. 2*, ed. G. H. Anderson and T. F. Transky (Grand Rapids, MI: Eerdmans, 1975), 51.

21. "Don't Know Mind," http://emptygatezen.com/teaching/2014/10/24/dont-know-mind.

11. PRACTICING RESURRECTION

1. Wendell Berry, *The Mad Farmer Poems* (Berkeley, CA: Counterpoint, 2008), 12.

13. LEARNING THROUGH SEEING AND NAMING

1. Jack Mezirow, *Transformative Dimensions of Adult Learning* (San Francisco: Jossey-Bass, 1991); Nick Zepke and Linda Leach, "Contextualized Meaning Making: One Way of Rethinking Experiential Learning and Self-Directed Learning?" *Studies in Continuing Education* 24, no. 2 (November 2002): 205–17.
2. Patricia Hill Collins and Sirma Bilge, *Intersectionality* (Cambridge: Polity, 2016), 11.
3. Kimberlé Crenshaw is often rightly credited with introducing the term "intersectionality" into the academic mainstream through two seminal articles. The controversy, however, is in regard to when the *concept* was first used by the academy. Some argue that female scholars of color had already begun to utilize intersectional analysis—even if they did not articulate it as such—to push back on generalizing experiences for women and for normalizing men's experiences for all. See Kimberlé Crenshaw, "Demarginalizing the Intersection of Race and Sex: A Black Feminist Critique of Antidiscrimination Doctrine, Feminist Theory and Antiracist Politics," *University of Chicago Legal Forum* 1, no. 8 (1989): 139–67, http://chicagounbound.uchicago.edu/uclf/ vol1989/iss1/8; "Mapping the Margins: Intersectionality, Identity Politics, and Violence against Women of Color," *Stanford Law Review* 43, no. 6 (July 1991): 1241–99, https://jstor.org/stable/1229039; Collins and Bilge, *Intersectionality*, 68–69; Ange-Marie Hancock, *Intersectionality: An Intellectual History* (New York: Oxford University Press, 2016), 38–40; Patricia R. Grzanka, *Intersectionality: A Foundations and Frontiers Reader* (Boulder, CO: Westview, 2014), xiv.
4. *Simultaneity* is an important concept for the theory. It is the idea that each identifier is always present and, therefore, should be considered for analysis. A person is not only a racial, gendered, or sexual person. They are all of these at once, not in parallel fashion but in intersecting manner. The context might highlight one of the person's identities over others, but this does not preclude other identifiers as they are experienced in life or in analysis.
5. Mark Chung Hearn, "Positionality, Intersectionality, and Power: Socially Locating the Higher Education Teacher in Multicultural Education," *Multicultural Education Review* 4, no. 2 (March 2015): 38–59.
6. People use intersectionality as a tool to analyze life, including identity construction. Intersectionality and identity, the primary way I utilize the theory here ("intersectional identities"), looks to expand our understanding of people, particularly as it has to do with not only the lived experience but also the political analysis of those intersecting identities. See Collins and Bilge, *Intersectionality*, 89.
7. I raised this example during an academic presentation on creating brave space for religious education, and a follow-up question posed was whether an academic educational space is the place for corporate prayer. My response is that if we do not allow students to live in, and reflect on, the tension-filled areas of our lives in a rather controlled and safe environment, how can we, as a school training religious and church professionals and leaders, honestly expect students to carry out their duties in increasingly pluralistic contexts that are less forgiving and generous, particularly with regard to faith and religious difference?
8. Positionality is similar to, and yet distinct from, intersectionality. Positionality is the social location in relation to others we assume in any given context due to our intersecting identities. My identity as a middle-aged father in a Korean American context is a social position different from that of a middle-aged mother.
9. While there are Evangelicals who are fundamentalist, these are not mutually inclusive of one another. Here, I understand fundamentalism ("If I am right, you are wrong" or its corollary, "If you are right, I am wrong") and dogmatism ("I have the corner on truth") as twin ideas that work together to prevent a person from holding well the ambiguity and complexity life offers, both of which are necessary for ministry and religious meaning making.
10. There are various evangelicalisms today despite what is portrayed in the media and popular culture, which strengthens the argument for intersectionality theory. Some resources on the diversity of Evangelicals include Deborah Jian Lee, *Rescuing Jesus: How People of Color, Women, and Queer Christians Are Reclaiming Evangelicalism* (Boston: Beacon, 2015); Tom Krattenmaker, *The Evangelicals You Don't Know: Introducing the Next Generation of Chris-*

tians (New York: Rowman & Littlefield, 2013); Soong-Chan Rah, *The Next Evangelicalism: Freeing the Church from Western Cultural Captivity* (Downers Grove, IL: Intervarsity, 2009). These three more popular resources are buffered by more academic resources, such as Randall Balmer, *Evangelicalism in America* (Waco, TX: Baylor University Press, 2016); Mark Noll, *The Scandal of the Evangelical Mind* (Grand Rapids, MI: William B. Eerdmans, 1994). See also https://crcc.usc.edu/report/the-varieties-of-american-evangelicalism/.

11. I have also needed to navigate various power conflicts because of others' micro-aggressions with regard to race, paternalism, and religious identity. While having to deal with any one of these axes is problematic, seeing them together through intersectionality theory deeply complexifies the matter.

12. Emmanuel Y. Lartey, *In Living Color: An Intercultural Approach to Pastoral Care and Counseling*, 2nd ed. (London: Jessica Kingsley, 2003), 34.

13. Ibid., 172.

14. Emile M. Townes, "Making the Way Together," in *Spotlight on Theological Education: Intersectionality in Theological Education*, ed. Jeanne Stevenson-Moessner, American Academy of Religion (April 2015): 4.

15. New Revised Standard Version.

14. THANK YOU FOR SEEING ME

1. All names have been changed.

17. LEARNING THROUGH OUR BODIES

1. Joy Harjo, "A Map of the Next World," as quoted in Becky Thompson, *Teaching with Tenderness: Toward an Embodied Practice* (Urbana: University of Illinois Press, 2017), 1.

2. While an exhaustive investigation of Descartes's philosophy is beyond the scope of this paper, see the online *Stanford Encyclopedia of Philosophy*, https://plato.stanford.edu/entries/descartes/.

3. Jaco J. Hamman, *Growing Down: Theology and Human Nature in the Virtual Age* (Waco, TX: Baylor University Press, 2017), 127.

4. Ibid., 127

5. Ibid., 127.

6. See Kevin Rathunde, "Montessori and Embodied Education," in *Alternative Education for the 21st Century: Philosophies, Approaches, Visions*, ed. Phillip A. Woods and Glenys J. Woods (New York: Palgrave Macmillan, 2009), 189–208.

7. Becky Thompson, *Teaching with Tenderness: Toward an Embodied Practice* (Urbana: University of Illinois Press, 2017), 36.

8. Ibid., 111.

9. M. Shawn Copeland, *Enfleshing Freedom: Body, Race, and Being* (Minneapolis: Fortress, 2010), 24.

10. Merriam-Webster defines idealism as "a theory that ultimate reality lies in a realm transcending phenomena." Phenomena references the sensory experienced, material world. Consider how idealism resonates with cultural perfectionism. https://www.merriam-webster.com/dictionary/idealism.

11. Mayra Rivera, "Carnal Corporeality: Tensions in Continental and Caribbean Thought," *Concordia: International Journal of Philosophy* 63 (2013), mayrarivera.com/files/mayrarivera/files/carnal_corporeality-concordia.pdf.

12. Ibid.

13. Mayra Rivera, *Poetics of the Flesh* (Durham, NC: Duke University Press, 2015), 2.

14. See Michelle Alexander, *The Cradle to Prison Pipeline* (New York: The New Press, 2012).

15. A former student wrote these aspects of being human in one word as a way of claiming a holistic theological anthropology. I am grateful for this creative insight.

16. Marcia Mount Shoop, *Let the Bones Dance: Embodiment and the Body of Christ* (Louisville, KY: Westminster John Knox, 2010), 11–12.

17. Ibid., 17–18.

18. Malou Juelskjaer, Thomas Moser, and Theresa Schilhab, eds., "Introduction," in *Learning Bodies* (Copenhagen: Danish School of Education Press, 2008), 7.

19. Ibid., 2.

20. Karen Barbour, "Beyond 'Somatophobia': Phenomenology and Movement Research in Dance," *Junctures: The Journal for Thematic Dialogue* 4 (June 2005): 35, https://junctures.org/index.php/junctures/article/view/140/144.

21. Susan Bordo, *The Unbearable Weight: Feminism, Western Culture, and the Body* (Berkeley: University of California Press, 1993), 6.

22. Ibid., 13–14.

23. For information on implicit/unconscious bias research, see Jennifer Eberhardt, *Biased: Uncovering the Hidden Prejudices That Shape What We See, Think, and Do* (New York: Penguin, 2019).

24. Thompson, *Teaching with Tenderness*, 13.

25. Ibid., 24.

26. Ibid., 3–6.

27. Ibid., 7–8.

28. Ibid., 10.

29. Trauma theory, contested in medical and academic circles (highlighting critiques of its Western lens and engaging postcolonial criticism), is an important, evolving lens in furthering our understanding of our bodies' role in construction of knowledge. See Anushka Pai, Alina M. Suris, and Carol S. North, "Posttraumatic Stress Disorder in the *DSM-5*: Controversy, Change, and Conceptual Considerations," *Behavioral Sciences (Basel, Switzerland)* 7, no. 1 (February 13, 2017), https://doi.org/10.3390/bs7010007; Susannah Radstone, Janet Walker, and Noah Shenk, "Trauma Theory," *Oxford Bibliographies* (2013), https://doi.org/10.1093/OBO/9780199791286-0147.

30. Ibid., 5.

31. Ibid., 18.

32. Ibid., 38.

33. Ibid., 25–53.

34. The term "learning contexts," rather than "placements" or "internships," for me, connotes more clearly the purpose of experiential pedagogy.

35. This can become an exercise in analyzing how space invites and discourages bodily presence. While meeting in alternative spaces requires flexibility and planning, it serves as an exercise in embodied reflection on the ways space influences learning and teaching.

36. Given the popular meaning the word "vulnerability" holds in our culture—weakness—I hesitate and yet must acknowledge that engaging bodies calls us to be vulnerable, permeable to one another. It is interesting to note that the etymology of the word "vulnerable" rests in the late Latin meaning of woundedness, in which we all share. https://www.etymonline.com/word/vulnerable.

37. Thompson, *Teaching with Tenderness*, 16.

38. Ibid., 18.

20. BREATHING INTO BEING

1. Leslie Feinberg, *Transgender Warriors: Making History from Joan of Arc to Dennis Rodman* (Boston: Beacon, 1997).

21. LEARNING THROUGH OUR COMMUNITY

1. Desmond Mpilo Tutu, *No Future without Forgiveness* (New York: Random House/Doubleday, 1999), 31.
2. David Hogue cautions against romanticizing or stereotyping either Western individualism or Eastern *communitas*, even as we honor the communities and cultures that have informed this perspective on being human. He insists on the importance of both *being* ourselves and *belonging* in various communities and how these interrelate. See David Hogue, "Because We Are: Practical Theology, Intersubjectivity and the Human Brain," in *Practicing Ubuntu: Practical Theological Perspectives on Injustice, Personhood and Human Dignity*, ed. Jaco Dreyer, Yolanda Dryer, Edward Foley, and Malan Nel (Münster, Germany: Lit Verlag, 2017), 181–91.
3. Daniel J. Siegel, *The Developing Mind: How Relationships and the Brain Interact to Shape Who We Are*, 2nd ed. (New York: Guilford, 2012), 3.
4. Daniel J. Siegel, *Pocket Guide to Interpersonal Neurobiology: An Integrative Handbook of the Mind* (New York: W. W. Norton, 2012), 4-1 through 4-7. This book is structured as a set of mutually implicating chapters and does not use a typical "page number" format.
5. Ibid., 4-4.
6. Ibid., 4-4.
7. Ibid., 22-1 through 22-5. See also Daniel J. Siegel, *Mindsight: The New Science of Personal Transformation* (New York: Random House/Bantam, 2011).
8. Allison Aubrey, "Feeling Anxious? Here's a Quick Tool to Center Your Soul," https://www.npr.org/2020/02/03/802347757/a-conversation-with-tara-brach-mindfulness-tools-for-big-feelings. This is an interview with Tara Brach about her book *Radical Compassion: Learning to Love Yourself and Your World with the Practice of RAIN* (New York: Random House/Viking, 2019).
9. Justin Reed, "Life's Not Fair," Spring Convocation, Louisville Presbyterian Theological Seminary, February 6, 2020.
10. Parker Palmer, *The Courage to Teach: Exploring the Inner Landscape of a Teacher's Life*, Tenth Anniversary Edition (San Francisco: Jossey-Bass, 1998, 2007).
11. Paolo Freire, *Pedagogy of the Oppressed*, trans. Myra Ramos (New York: Continuum, 2007).
12. Palmer, *The Courage to Teach*, 95.
13. Ibid., 95.
14. Ibid., 104, 106.
15. Ibid., 106.
16. See Johnson and Gatewood's chapter in this volume.
17. See Cook and Mayfield's chapter in this volume.
18. Brené Brown, *Daring Greatly: How the Courage to Be Vulnerable Transforms the Way We Live, Love, Parent, and Lead* (New York: Random House/Avery, 2012), 37.
19. Ibid., 2.
20. Ibid., 45.
21. Brené Brown, *Dare to Lead: Brave Work. Tough Conversations. Whole Hearts.* (New York: Random House, 2018).
22. Ibid., 143.
23. Ibid., 145.
24. Ibid., 145.
25. Ibid., 147.
26. Ibid., 148. It is important to acknowledge that North American society remains more accepting of anger from white men than from people of color or women. See Trina Jones and Kimberly Jane Norwood, "Aggressive Encounters & White Fragility: Deconstructing the Trope of the Angry Black Woman," *Iowa Law Review* 102 (2017): 2017–69.
27. Brown, *Dare to Lead*, 149.
28. See bell hooks, *Teaching to Transgress: Education as the Practice of Freedom* (New York: Routledge, 1994), chapter 6, "Essentialism and Experience."
29. hooks, *Teaching to Transgress*, 91–92.

30. Ibid., 90–91.
31. Ibid., 92
32. Ibid., 92.
33. Brian Arao and Kristi Clemens, "From Safe Spaces to Brave Spaces: A New Way to Frame Dialogue around Diversity and Social Justice," in *The Art of Effective Facilitation: Reflections from Social Justice Educators*, ed. Lisa M. Landreman (Sterling, VA: Stylus, 2013), 135–50. I am grateful to my colleague Rev. Dr. Christine Hong of Columbia Theological Seminary for pointing me toward this chapter several years ago.
34. Ibid., 139.
35. Ibid., 139. Parker Palmer writes about this kind of transformative authentic learning, which stretches and grows one's capacity to love others, in chapter 3 of *The Courage to Teach*, when he addresses the pain that comes with learning and changing.
36. Ibid., 143.
37. Ibid., 143.
38. Arao and Clemens, "Brave Space," 143.
39. Ibid., 145.
40. Ibid., 145.
41. Ibid., 146.
42. Ibid., 147.
43. Ibid., 148.
44. Jones originally published this poem on her website. However, at the time of writing, her website was inaccessible. This version of the poem was found at https://onbeing.org/wp-content/uploads/2019/10/An-Invitation-to-Brave-Space.pdf.
45. See this article by Stephanie P. Jones, "Ending Curriculum Violence," *Teaching Tolerance* 64 (Spring 2020).
46. Palmer, *The Courage to Teach*, 87.

22. INTRODUCING THEOLOGICAL EDUCATION THROUGH THE INTERSECTION OF BIBLE AND PASTORAL CARE

1. As a Presbyterian Church (USA) seminary, Louisville offers four degree programs (MDiv, MAR, MA in Marriage and Family Therapy, and DMin). Historically, the seminary was a bridge between northern and southern Presbyterians; we continue this legacy today through our focus on ministry across differences (racial, sexual, theological, etc.).
2. Eboo Patel, *Acts of Faith* (Boston: Beacon, 2007).
3. Cari Jackson, *The Gift to Listen: The Courage to Hear* (Minneapolis: Augsburg Fortress, 2003).
4. Adapted from Emma J. Justes, *Hearing Beyond the Words: How to Become a Listening Pastor* (Nashville: Abingdon, 2006), 42–43.
5. Nelle Morton, *The Journey Is Home* (Boston: Beacon, 1985), 127.
6. Denise Dombkowski Hopkins and Michael Koppel, *Grounded in the Living Word: The Old Testament and Pastoral Care Practices* (Grand Rapids, MI: Eerdmans, 2010), 19.
7. Frederick C. Tiffany and Sharon H. Ringe, *Biblical Interpretation: A Roadmap* (Nashville: Abingdon, 1996), 120–21.
8. Howard Gardner, *Frames of Mind: The Theory of Multiple Intelligences* (New York: Basic Books, 1993).
9. Patricia O'Connell Killen and John de Beer, *The Art of Theological Reflection* (New York: Crossroad, 1994), viii.
10. Killen and de Beer, *The Art of Theological Reflection*, ix.
11. Ibid., 5, 10, 17.
12. See Howard W. Stone and James O. Duke, *How to Think Theologically*, 3rd ed. (Minneapolis: Fortress, 2013) and Carrie Doehring, *The Practice of Pastoral Care: A Postmodern Approach*, revised and expanded ed. (Louisville, KY: Westminster John Knox, 2015).

23. PROVIDENTIAL FRIENDSHIP

1. Gerrard Manley Hopkins, *Poems and Prose* (New York: Penguin, 1985), 51.

Index

authority shift, 20, 75

brave space, 138–140

calling: and mentoring, 57–58; and self-discovery, 30–32
conversation: intentional, 153; sustained by, 150
critical reflection, 37, 40

embodied epistemology, 91
emotional maturity, 52
empathy, 136–138
epistemic humility, 137

feedback: and reflection, 8
feminism: definition, 19

imagination: pastoral, 5, 152; and understanding, 40; use of, 10
intersectionality, 82–83; and expanding the circle of learning, 6; and multiplicity, 86; and positionality, 84, 167n8; and simultaneity, 83; and specificity, 87; and totality, 99; as a way of seeing me and others, 94

learning community, 153, 154, 158, 162
learning cycle, 14, 145, 165n3
learning theories: behaviorist, 1; cognitive, 1; communal, 92; constructivist, 2, 36; embodied, 112–114; experiential, 8–13; transformative, 63
listening: holy, 45–46; importance of, 144; instead of leading, 26; and learning, 121; patient and intentional, 93

meaning making, 35–37, 81

narrative, storytelling: curating the, 6, 39–40; and future action, 42; and invitation, 41–42; and overcoming differences, 46; power of, 38–39

pedagogy of tenderness, 108, 112–114; definition, 113

Scriptures: misuse and misinterpretation, 18
somatophobia, 109

transformation: and careful planning of the course, 20; and story-sharing, 47

ubuntu, 134
unlearning : and don't-know mind, 63–64; as learning, 59–60; and letting go of prior knowledge, 4, 61–62, 74, 77, 103, 124; as relearning, 67–68

vulnerability: collective, 129; definition, 169n36; and empathy, 133; and gaining trust, 18; and theological education, 146

About the Contributors

Paulina Alvarado, native of Chile, is a Catholic lay minister of the archdiocese of Seattle and a Seattle University graduate with a master of arts in pastoral studies. Her faith, her personal history, and her professional experience as a victim advocate and lay minister give depth to her professional, spiritual, and artistic vocation. She currently serves as a chaplain resident at Saint Joseph Medical Center in Tacoma, Washington.

Jennifer Bashaw (PhD Fuller Theological Seminary, MDiv Truett Seminary, BA Baylor) is assistant professor of New Testament and Christian ministry at Campbell University in North Carolina. Her scholarship focuses on the disciplines of homiletics, New Testament studies, and practical ministry. She and her husband, Kerry, have three sons—Noah, Riley, and Isaac—and she is an ordained minister in the American Baptist Churches, USA.

Erika Tobin Bergh is a fun-loving Evangelical Lutheran Church in America pastor and a proud member of the low-waste living and bi communities. She is currently serving at Christ Our Savior Lutheran Church in Anchorage, Alaska, where she lives with her husband and their two cats.

Christin Bothe is currently a Reality Ministries Fellow in Durham, North Carolina. She earned a BA from Hope College and recently finished her MTS at Duke Divinity School. Her education and work have been grounded in the life of the North Street Neighborhood in Durham, North Carolina, a community of friends with and without intellectual and developmental disabilities.

About the Contributors

Sung Hee Chang serves on the faculty of Union Presbyterian Seminary as associate professor of supervised ministry and director of supervised ministry and vocational planning on the Charlotte campus. Previously, she had served as an educator in several churches in Virginia and North Carolina. Her areas of special interest include curriculum theory with particular attention to contextual education, postcolonial studies, intercultural theological education, and ecumenical formation.

Carol J. Cook is the Harrison Ray Anderson Professor Emerita of Pastoral Theology at Louisville Presbyterian Theological Seminary.

Katie Crowe is senior pastor of Trinity Avenue Presbyterian Church in Durham, North Carolina. A graduate of Berry College, Katie received her master of divinity from Princeton Theological Seminary and doctor of ministry in Reformed Christian Spirituality from Pittsburgh Theological Seminary. Prior to serving at Trinity Avenue, Katie completed a clinical pastoral education residency at Robert Wood Johnson University Hospital in New Brunswick, New Jersey, and served as associate pastor for local and global mission at First Presbyterian Church in Charlotte, cofounding the Charlotte chapter of Contemplative Outreach, dedicated to furthering the practice of centering prayer. Katie and her husband, Rob, enjoy life with their son, Dillon, and two boxers.

Rev. Angela Denise Davis, MDiv, MS, is an ordained minister, public speaker, activist, and community ukulele teacher. Her work as a minister centers on the fusion of art and spirituality to enrich the ways we move in personal and social spaces. As a blind black lesbian, her public speaking centers around justice issues located at the intersection of race, class, gender, sexual orientation, and disability. Her call is to facilitate conversations and theological reflections along the fence line of those differences. She challenges her audiences to wrestle with the difficult and to support each other's journey into new territory. She is the founder of Uke Griot, a program to awaken musical skills in adults; of Sister Harriet, a spiritual collective for queer women; and creator of ZAMI NOBLA Podcast.

Damien Pascal Domenack, MDiv, is pursuing a secondary ThM at Vanderbilt Divinity School. Damien is a santero priest whose ministry centers transgender, queer, black and brown, and immigrant communities of which he is a part. His research focuses on Afro-Latinx diasporic dance as embodied prayer. Damien is a prison abolitionist and a founding member of Audre Lorde Project's TransJustice in New York City.

Abigale Embry is a bereavement coordinator and chaplain at a nonprofit inpatient hospice in Virginia.

Matthew Floding is director of ministerial formation at Duke Divinity School. He has served as a theological field educator since 1999, following service as pastor and college chaplain. He is editor and contributor to *Welcome to Theological Field Education!* and *Engage: A Theological Field Education Toolkit* and coeditor and contributor to *Empower: A Toolkit for Supervisor-Mentors in Theological Field Education*. He is coeditor of the journal *Reflective Practice: Formation and Supervision in Ministry* and is a past chair of the Association for Theological Field Education.

Tee S. Gatewood III is the pastor of Arbor Dale Presbyterian Church in Banner Elk, North Carolina. He holds a masters in New Testament from Regent College in Vancouver, British Columbia, and a PhD in theology from the University of St Andrews, Scotland.

Val Goins is the pastor of Glendale United Methodist Church and is completing a residency in clinical chaplaincy at the Robley Rex Veterans Hospital in Louisville, Kentucky.

Franklin Golden is the founding pastor of Durham Presbyterian Church. He lives in Hillsborough, North Carolina, where he builds guitars in the woods while thinking about what he might say on Sunday morning.

Rev. Mark Chung Hearn, PhD, is director and assistant clinical professor of contextual education and ministry at Seattle University. He is the son of Korean immigrant parents and has worked as a pastor, consultant, and collegiate volleyball coach. He has published on the social construction of Korean American men, antioppression, and sports and spirituality.

Rev. Dr. Trygve D. Johnson is the Hinga Boersma Dean of the Chapel of Hope College. He holds an MDiv from Western Theological Seminary and a PhD in theology from University of St Andrews, Scotland, and is ordained in the Reformed Church in America. He is author of *The Preacher as Liturgical Artist* and speaks widely on college campuses and churches around the country.

Rev. Marc Antoine Lavarin serves as the assistant to the pastor for young adults and online ministry at the historic Alfred Street Baptist Church in Alexandria, Virginia, under the leadership of Rev. Dr. Howard-John Wesley. Rev. Lavarin completed his undergraduate studies at Northeastern University. He was selected to be a member of the 2013 Teach for America Massachusetts cohort. Rev. Lavarin earned his master of education degree from Boston University and completed his master of divinity degree at Duke University in 2018. He was ordained at the Evangelical First Haitian Baptist Church of Worcester, Massachusetts, under the direction of his father, Rev. Antoine Lavarin. In addition to his ministerial role, Rev. Lavarin currently serves on the steering committee for the Alexandria, Virginia, Equal Justice Initiative.

Tyler D. Mayfield is the A. B. Rhodes Professor of Old Testament at Louisville Presbyterian Theological Seminary and author of *Unto Us a Child Is Born: Isaiah, Advent, and Our Jewish Neighbors*.

Sandra Monroe earned her master of divinity at Louisville Presbyterian Theological Seminary and is currently a staff chaplain at SSM Health/St. Louis University Hospital in St. Louis, Missouri.

Joyce del Rosario is an assistant professor in the practice of ministry for the Pacific School of Religion. After over 15 years of full-time ministry experience in faith-based nonprofit work, Joyce now teaches field education, social transformation in action, social justice field work, and immersions. Her research interests also include Filipino American theology, children at risk, and womanist theology.

Lindsay Ross-Hunt is an Episcopal priest and campus chaplain at Western Washington University in Bellingham, Washington.

Rev. Erik Samuelson, MA, MDiv, is an Evangelical Lutheran Church in America pastor, leadership and vocational discernment coach, practical theological educator, and trainer in community organizing, coaching, and spiritual practices. Erik's passion is to help people and organizations connect deeply to what makes them come alive and to accompany them on their journeys of transformation.

Trudy Hawkins Stringer is assistant professor of the practice of ministry and associate director of field education at Vanderbilt University Divinity School. She teaches at the intersections of theology and practice, utilizing experiential pedagogy to inform theological inquiry and construction. Her interests include embodiment, justice, and theological meaning making, as well as interprofessional teaching and learning. She is an ordained elder in the United Methodist Church and served as a hospital chaplain for 13 years.

Marijke Strong is a pastor, coach, spiritual director, and writer. She currently oversees the Canadian churches of the Reformed Church in America and coaches with The Leader's Journey, an organization that offers coaching and consulting toward wholehearted leadership. She loves to do anything outdoors, to read, make art, travel, build community, and work collaboratively toward reconciliation and restoration. Her latest project is coleading The Still Point Community, a group of people who are deconstructing and reconstructing mental models of faith and life. Marijke lives in Hamilton, Ontario.

Rev. Dr. Leslie Veen is director of contextual education and lecturer at Pacific Lutheran Theological Seminary. Dr. Veen has a deep love for helping people to grow in their faith in God and in their sense of calling as baptized children of God. Drawing on her work as a Spanish instructor, seminary staff and faculty member, and parish associate with Seventh Avenue Presbyterian Church in San Francisco, as well as on her advanced studies in Christian spirituality, Dr. Veen helps students explore many areas of practical theology that come to into play as they seek to be leaders of faith communities.

Allison Waters lives in Durham, North Carolina, where she is the clinical director of Reality Ministries, a community of belonging where people of all abilities share life together. She has a master of social work from University of North Carolina at Chapel Hill and a master of divinity from Duke Divinity School. She specializes in utilizing clinical and theological training to empower faith-based communities to truly embrace neurodiversity and extend welcome to people with intellectual and developmental difficulties. Allison loves the beach, a delicious meal, stand-up comedy, and her dog, Crinkle.

Shaina Williams is a San Francisco Bay Area native with a passion for helping women and children in need. She has a bachelor degree in psychology from Northwest University and is in her final year of completing her master of divinity at Seattle University's School of Theology and Ministry.

William Willimon is a bishop in the United Methodist Church. He served as the dean of Duke Chapel and professor of Christian ministry at Duke University for 20 years. He returned to Duke after serving as the bishop of the North Alabama Conference from 2004 to 2012. Willimon is the author of 70 books, and in 2017 he published *Who Lynched Willie Earle? Confronting Racism through Preaching.*

www.ingramcontent.com/pod-product-compliance
Lightning Source LLC
Chambersburg PA
CBHW020739230426
43665CB00009B/491